HELEN MACFARLANE

Raya Dunayevskaya Series in Marxism and Humanism

Series Editors: Kevin B. Anderson, Purdue University
Olga Domanski, News and Letters Committees
Peter Hudis, News and Letters Committees

The Power of Negativity: Selected Writings on the Dialectic in Hegel and Marx
Edited and Introduced by Peter Hudis and Kevin B. Anderson
Philosophy and Revolution: From Hegel to Sartre and from Marx to Mao
by Raya Dunayevskaya
Helen MacFarlane: A Feminist, Revolutionary Journalist, and Philosopher in Mid-Nineteenth-Century England
by David Black

HELEN MACFARLANE

A Feminist, Revolutionary Journalist, and Philosopher in Mid-Nineteenth-Century England

David Black

LEXINGTON BOOKS

Lanham • Boulder • New York • Toronto • Oxford

LEXINGTON BOOKS

Published in the United States of America
by Lexington Books
An imprint of The Rowman & Littlefield Publishing Group, Inc.
4501 Forbes Boulevard, Suite 200, Lanham, Maryland 20706

PO Box 317
Oxford
OX2 9RU, UK

British Library Cataloguing in Publication Information Available

Library of Congress Cataloging-in-Publication Data

Black, David, 1950–
  Helen Macfarlane : a feminist, revolutionary journalist, and philosopher in
mid-nineteenth-century England / David Black.
      p. cm. — (Raya Dunayevskaya series in Marxism and humanism)
  Includes Macfarlane's original translation of The Communist Manifesto.
  Includes index.
  ISBN 0-7391-0863-8 (cloth : alk. paper) — ISBN 0-7391-0864-6 (pbk. : alk. paper)
    1. Macfarlane, Helen. 2. Women revolutionaries—Great Britain—Biography.
3. Communism—Great Britain—History—19th century. 4. Chartism. I. Marx,
Karl, 1818–1883. Manifest der Kommunist-ischen Partei. English. II. Title. III.
Series
HQ1595.M32B56 2004
335.4′092—dc22   2004012770

Printed in the United States of America

♾™ The paper used in this publication meets the minimum requirements of
American National Standard for Information Sciences—Permanence of Paper
for Printed Library Materials, ANSI/NISO Z39.48-1992.

Contents

Acknowledgments

I acknowledge the British Library, Hyde Park Family History Centre, Marx Memorial Library, Public Record Office, Family Records Centre (National Archives), South Place Ethical Society, and the Women's Library.

Thanks also to Virginia Clark, Jim Clayson, and Christopher P. Ford for their kind help and encouragement; and to Lexington editors Robert Carley and Deborah F. Justice for their support. All responsibility for the text is mine.

Introduction

In 1848, as the February Revolution in France unleashed a chain of insurrection across Continental Europe, the Chartist movement in England once more took to the streets. For the third time since 1838, a petition was presented to Parliament for electoral reform and universal male suffrage; and when the House of Commons rejected it, the middle-class allies of the Chartists backed off once again from a confrontation with the government. Isolated uprisings broke out in parts of the country, but were easily suppressed by troops and special constables. Chartist leader and member of Parliament for Nottingham, Feargus O'Connor, drew the lesson from the defeat that the six-point "People's Charter" needed to be watered down in order to maintain the movement's alliance with the Manchester Liberals. Chartist radicals, such as George Julian Harney, on the other hand, saw in the defeat one betrayal too many. The radicals argued for a new independent working-class movement with a "social" and internationalist perspective. To this end Harney, in June 1849, launched a new monthly, the *Democratic Review of British Politics, History and Literature*; in spring 1850, he resigned from O'Connor's paper, the *Northern Star* to set up a new rival weekly, the *Red Republican*. In November 1850, Harney published a translation of *The Communist Manifesto* in his paper, presenting it to his readers as "the most revolutionary document ever given to the world."

In a biography of Harney published in 1958, A. R. Schoyen noted that one of the most prolific contributors to his presses, who wrote under the name of Howard Morton, showed a remarkable understanding of what would later become known as Marxism. Schoyen's probing into the identity of this mysterious person led him to ask:

> Who could this be, but Helen Macfarlane, the admired acquaintance of Marx and Engels and translator of the first printed English version of the *Communist Manifesto*, which appeared in the four November 1850 issues of the *Red Republican*?

Schoyen's statement has never been seriously challenged and, until now, has never been followed up as the important discovery it was. Macfarlane was of that generation of post–Napoleonic War "baby boomers," which included other original and radical women writers such as George Eliot (Mary Ann Evans) and the Brontë sisters. Like these literary contemporaries, Helen Macfarlane had to use a male nom de plume to get her work into print; but for her, an avowed feminist and revolutionary, the obscurity inflicted on her by bourgeois male society—and its historians—was to be near total.

Historians of Chartism have always bemoaned the fact that most Chartist activists, living in modest circumstances, did not have the luxury of keeping archives. Schoyen, on writing about Harney, says:

> The impersonal nature of most of the available materials on Julian Harney, mainly newspapers and periodicals in which he wrote, leave one with no more than conjecture about some aspects of his life.

Schoyen's words resound a lot more starkly in the case of Helen Macfarlane. Her life story, through no fault of her own, is more resistant to the "picklocks of biographers" than almost any other nineteenth-century writer of outstanding talent, even the notoriously obscure Isadore Ducasse (Comte de Lautréamont) author of *Les Chants de Maldoror*, who died during the Siege of Paris in 1870. One obvious reason for Macfarlane "keeping her head down" behind a male pseudonym must have been the daunting prejudice that would face any woman who openly expressed radical political opinions. When two generations earlier, in 1792, Mary Wollstonecraft published *A Vindication of the Rights of Woman* and went off to Paris to support the French Revolution, she had been attacked by Horace Walpole as a "hyena in petticoats." But even in 1850, British society, in Helen Macfarlane's judgment, condemned itself in "the position of women, who are regarded by law not as *persons* but as *things*, and placed in the same category as children and the insane." Just as the storming of the Bastille in 1789 had introduced the sansculotte into the demonology of English opinion, so the June Days of 1848 in Paris provided the equally terrifying figure of the "Red Cap" Republican, this time armed not only with the rifle and the pike but also with the "damnable doctrines" of socialism and communism. In early Victorian England, a female "Red Republican" who openly proved that she could wield the pen as a revolutionary weapon better than most men, would have been scourged as a danger to public order and decency.

Although I have been able to unearth some previously unknown biographical material on Macfarlane, most of her life story remains elusive; the problem is compounded by her sudden "disappearance" in 1851. Most of what has been discoverable about her comes from her published writings—twelve substantial essays in all—and some of the writings and correspondence of her associates, especially Harney, Engels and Marx. This book then, is necessarily and unashamedly, a *Biography of an Idea*.

Macfarlane was living in Vienna in 1848 when the Revolution against the Hapsburg monarchy radicalized her. Her fluency in the German language gave her access to the great philosophic works of German Idealism and its radical "Young Hegelian" inheritors, such as Heindrich Heine and Karl Marx. She was described by the latter as the most original of Harney's stable of writers; as a rara avis among the empiricist English. For Macfarlane, as for Hegel—and arguably Marx as well—the Idea of Freedom was identified with the Idea of History. Macfarlane was not only the first "British Marxist": she was also the first British commentator on Hegel's philosophy and the first translator of any of his words into English.

In the following text I begin with a look at the philosophic underpinnings of Macfarlane's view of British History as compared with those of the Labour Historians who have written "her" history—that is, the history of Chartism. Next, I provide some background on two main themes of Macfarlane's thought: firstly, the economic and political developments in England that informed Marx's analysis of class struggle in *The Communist Manifesto*; secondly, Hegel's Idea of Freedom and its "externalization" in the Age of Revolutions. I then look at the world of radical journalism that Macfarlane joined on returning to England and at what biographical material there is on Macfarlane herself. In Macfarlane's own writings, her polemical opponents included the Manchester Liberals, who fought against "Old Corruption" under the banner of Free Trade; the "rosewater political sentimentalists," Charles Dickens and Alphonse de Lamartine; and, most importantly, Thomas Carlyle. Whereas Carlyle associated democracy with the "Mob" and advocated a return to the feudal values of a "real aristocracy," Macfarlane's "narrative of history" saw a "pure democracy" emerging from class struggles. Macfarlane's narrative takes in the rebellious slaves of antiquity; the early Christians; the Lollards and other heretics of the Middle Ages; and finally Chartism and its potential for renewal as a socialist movement.

Like Marx, Macfarlane was influenced by the great French revolutionary, August Blanqui, for whom democracy was a historical process leading toward a "Republic without Helots." For Macfarlane, this meant a society "where freedom and equality will be the acknowledged birth right of every human being . . . without poor, without classes. . . . A society . . . not only of free men, but of free *women*."

In a period in which the Chartists were divided on whether "social" or "political" demands should come first, Macfarlane drew on the ideas of *The Communist Manifesto* to formulate a political program specifically suited to British conditions. In the immediate period, she argued, what was needed was a "double movement" of centralized Democratic action: the struggle for the Charter as a political reform and a "revolutionary and social propaganda" that would promote "critical insight into the conditions of real social movement," rather than the claims of competing factions and sects.

Macfarlane, like her contemporary George Eliot, turned to German philosophy to understand the growing crisis in Christianity. Hegel argued that despite Luther's great blow for freedom, Protestantism had introduced a "tormenting uncertainty" into the minds of individuals. Similarly, for Macfarlane, in the "doubt and fluctuation, of unrest, of weariness and vexation of soul—the region of protestantism . . . [there was] no fundamental principle, upon which a reasonable creature could find a firm footing." Protestantism was "a state of transition . . . the stepping stone for the human mind in its progress from deism to pantheism"; from "a belief in some things, in the divinity of one being or of one man, to a belief in the divinity of All beings." The "divine nature (or at least in a manifestation of it which is found only in man)" was, she argued, "common to us all." For Macfarlane, "the words Justice and Love" were not mere empty sounds without a meaning": rather, as in Sophocles' *Antigone*, they were "laws of God," which "are not of today, nor of yesterday," but "exist from all eternity."

In conclusion, I assess the significance of the historic encounter between Marx and the English Chartists, in which Helen Macfarlane played such a crucial part, and her originality as a revolutionary thinker.

1

Interrogating History

"Birds Eye View"

According to the "Constitutional" historians of the nineteenth century, the seed of Liberty was planted with the Magna Carta in 1215, and then grew through the Reformation and the revolutions of the seventeenth century, until finally flowering with the Parliamentary Reform Bill of 1832. An essay by Helen Macfarlane published in the *Democratic Review* in September 1850, titled "A Birds Eye View of the Glorious British Constitution," attacks this "Whig Interpretation" of history. Dismissing the "cant and twaddle about the wisdom of our ancestors, veneration of the past with its admirable institutions and the like," she asks, "When did this boasted constitution make its first appearance?" and "Who were its originators?"

> Wisdom of our ancestors? . . . Which set of ancestors? Of the Saxons? Then we shall make sad havoc of the Anglo-Normans. . . . The wisdom of the Puritans? Perhaps, all things considered, the most logical and least stupid of all our multifarious ancestors; yet I shudder to think what then became of the Stuarts and their adherents; not to mention the "worldly and profane" wisdom of Dutch William, and the treacherous, mean, sneaking, rascally aristocrats who placed him on the throne.[1]

"British history," she contends, "on being interrogated, gives a very different account of the matter" from that offered by the "advocates of the past." In tracing how British society came to be "defended by the gigantic fiction of the 'glorious British constitution,'" she points out that the "Lords" were "the lineal descendants of mail-clad Norman barbarians": the Norman King, or *roi*, needed a "consultation" with these "warrior chiefs" on "how to keep the '*subjecti*,' i.e., 'these base saxon dogs,' in proper subjection."

> The bulk of the nation, namely, the Saxons, were regarded after the Conquest "*come gens taillable et corvéable a merci*"—taxable, and forced to do the taskwork at the will of their masters. There is almost no mention of the vanquished for some time after the Conquest, except in Anglo-Norman charters, as "serfs, villains, colons," etcetera, who could acquire no property, and were sold along with houses, cattle, and farm implements, as belonging to the ground—"*vêtement de la terre*."

When Edward I called the "Model Parliament" in 1295, a number of burghs were "required to send deputies to the council of the king and his peers . . . for the purpose of declaring how much the inhabitants of their respective townships could pay without being utterly ruined." The expense of the "Commons" deputations was "so onerous for the burghs selected as the victims of royal avarice, that according to [David] Hume [in his *History of England*] 'no intelligence could be more disagreeable to any borough than to find that they must elect, or to any individual that he be elected.'"

> With this first appearance of the Third Estate, the "sacred and sacramental formula," . . . "kings, lords, and commons" achieved that "absurdity" of the "admirable balance of powers" which forms so distinguishing a feature in our venerable constitution. . . . Is this chimerical characteristic of our glorious constitution to be found later, for example in the seventeenth century, when the Commons cut off the king's head and kicked the lords to the devil? An odd balance of power, that?

The "British Constitution," as it stood in 1850, was "the collective epithet for the present system of class legislation . . . the glorious British Joint Stock Company for fleecing the starving producers of their last penny." The entire process of "reforms" had "only been quarrels between the two ruling classes—landed and manufacturing interests." The monarchy's role in the set-up had become negligible:

> The sovereign of these realms being notoriously a mere puppet in the hands of a profligate aristocratic clique; which, under the names of a Conservative or Whig administration thimbleriggs majorities in Parliament, and uses up the Proletarians for its own profit and that of the middle-classes who support the system because they share the plunder.[2]

Macfarlane's reading of British history is not just another attack on the usurpation of "Olde England" by the "Norman Yoke." Her analysis reveals her appropriation of the opening statement of *The Communist Manifesto*: "Hithertofore the history of Society has been the history of the battles between the classes composing it." In her words:

> From the earliest dawn of civilisation, from the first formation of society among the Caucasian races of man, we see nothing else going on than the struggles between classes or castes. In Hindostan and Egypt—the cradles of modern culture—we find class domination existing as a prominent, palpable, unmistakable fact. It has continued to be an historical fact down to our own times, under the almost infinite variety, obtaining in the aspects and degrees of civilization; and the battles of the social castes form the narrative of history.

Labour Histories

The "moderation" of the Fabian socialists who founded the school of Labour History in the 1890s was a far cry from the political and philosophical attitude expressed in the above "narrative of history." The pioneers of Labour History did not so much break with the "Whig" idea of "progress" as develop a socialist version of it: working-class history was seen as the forward march of political reformers, trade unions, and cooperative/self-help societies toward unity under a state-socialist parliamentary "Labour" party. The Chartists are portrayed in Sidney and Beatrice Webb's *History of Trade Unionism* as "fustian orators" and "pretentious and incompetent leaders." Apart from a few "moderate" exceptions, the Chartist leaders, with their "political and economic quackery," had "disgraced" the cause of progress and alienated respectable opinion.[3]

Twentieth-century Marxist Labour Historians took a more sympathetic view of Chartism. They argued that despite the historical "immaturity" of the class forces comprising the movement —artisans and small producers steeped in "petit bourgeois" ideologies such as Jacobinism and Utopian Socialism—there were tendencies within it who prefigured the ideas of "scientific socialism." In this "materialist" conception of history, in which "ideology" is seen as determined by the development of productive forces, socialist theory could only have taken hold once Britain, as the first capitalist country, had produced a large enough industrial working-class and a scientifically minded intelligentsia. That explained why, according to John Strachey, Chartism had failed to develop a "realistic economic theory" and program for bringing the means of production under state control, "according to a predetermined plan."[4]

In the 1970s, Gareth Stedman-Jones and various colleagues on the *New Left Review* began to challenge the "old schools" of Labour History. Stedman-Jones's 1972 essay, "The Poverty of Empiricism," attacks the conceptions of even the most sophisticated Marxist historians as being "ultimately homologous to the old liberal idea of progress." Like the early Marx they had attempted to ground and verify the "values" of interpretation in "the immanent movement of history itself," a position that could only lock the historian into "an unreal debate" about "whether there is progress, and thus whether there is meaning and direction in history." As an alternative to the humanism of the early Marx, Stedman-Jones offers the "structuralist Marxism" of Louis Althusser, which contends that "there is no such thing as history in general" but only "specific structures which have specific histories."[5] In attempting to conceptualize the "specific structures" of Chartism, Stedman-Jones suggests that the movement represented not so much immature working-class ideology as a "popular radicalism," which from the 1770s to the 1860s was held together by the grievance that too much power lay in too few hands.

Certainly, the factory owners, radicals, and workers of Lancashire could and often did find common cause as the "industrious classes" taking on "Old Corruption." In 1815, Parliament pushed through a new Corn Law that prohibited the import of grain until domestic prices had reached eighty shillings a quarter. The resulting rise in bread prices, combined with the economic disruption caused by the end of the Napoleonic War, united urban opinion against the landowner-dominated Parliament. But the anti-landowner alliance, as we shall see, proved to be highly unstable as the struggle between labor and capital intensified in the first half of the nineteenth century.

Notes

1. *Democratic Review*, September 1850. *Democratic Review of British Politics, History and Literature 1849–50*, ed. G. J. Harney (London: Merlin, 1990).

2. *Red Republican*, June 22, 1850. *The Red Republican & The Friend of the People: London 1850–51*. Facsimile reprint. Introduction by John Saville (London: Merlin, 1966).

3. Quoted in John Strachey, *Theory and Practice of Socialism* (London: Left Book Club, 1936), 349–50.

4. Strachey, *Theory*, 345.

5. Gareth Stedman-Jones, "The Poverty of Empiricism," in *Ideology and Social Science*, ed. R. Blackburn (London: Fontana, 1972). "Utopian Socialism Reconsidered," in *People's History and Socialist Theory*, ed. R Samuel (London: History Workshop Series, 1981).

2

The Making of
Red Republicanism

Popular Radicalism and Class-Consciousness

As the Napoleonic War drew to a close, class struggle in some
industrial areas of England took the form of "Luddism." Such
was the distress caused by the introduction of labor-saving machinery and the import of cheap shoddy goods that workers
smashed the machines in the factories and burned the "shod-
dies" at the dockside. In 1811 and 1812 the government deployed
twelve thousand troops in the North and Midlands to put down
Luddite sabotage; King George III brought over from Germany
fifteen thousand of his Hessian guards in case they were needed.
After the war ended, an upsurge in mass protest for parliamentary reform culminated in the Peterloo Massacre of 1819 in Manchester.

Throughout the first quarter of the century, the Lancashire
cotton industry was beset by a structural imbalance between
mechanized yarn spinning and a weaving process still carried
out by home-workers. The weavers suffered from a constant
downward pressure on their living standards due to foreign
competition: weavers on the Continent, utilizing English-spun
cotton, were fed more cheaply in the absence of the English-
style Corn Laws. In 1825, overproduction brought on the first

general capitalist crisis, with suspension of investments, followed by sackings and wage-cuts on a massive scale.[1] With the repeal of the Combination Acts in 1825, the trade unionists began to debate political economy in their *Trades Newspaper* and in radical publications such as the *Black Dwarf*. Whereas previously political radicals had focused on taxation and currency manipulation as the causes of distress, the new problems thrown up by machino-facture shifted attention to the increased exploitation of labor and the "anarchy" of competition. E. P. Thompson says that these debates indicate a "complete rupture" between middle-class Utilitarianism and an emergent "trade union theory" over "the wedding which had been solemnized, in the pages of James Mill, between Malthusianism and political economy."[2] The Malthusian argument, that workers, rather than fight the employer class, should restrict their numbers so as not to "overstock the demand for labourers," had some support among radicals, notably Francis Place. But trade union theory found a powerful exponent in the Mechanics Institute lecturer Thomas Hodgskin, who developed a pre-Marxian theory of exploitation in his book, *Labour Defended Against the Claims of Capital*, published anonymously in 1825. In investigating the implications of Adam Smith's argument that "labour is the source of all wealth," Hodgskin helped to turn it into a political slogan. The radical M.P. and cotton spinners' representative, John Fielden, argued in William Cobbett's *Register* for measures to protect workers' livelihoods, such as a statutory minimum wage, safety inspections, restrictions on working hours, and an elected board of trade to regulate industries hit by fluctuations in the market. This, he said, would spare political economists from the "mortification of having to complain any more of distress arising out of overproduction." In the 1830s and 1840s, as weaving became mechanized, there emerged a new disbalance: between cotton manufacture and other parts of the economy, especially agriculture and machine making. While the price of textile goods fell, wages resisted further devaluation because of rising food prices and the cost of machinery and land remained high. In the machine-making sector, engineering firms frequently overextended themselves, producing more machines than industry could absorb. As the industry lurched from crisis to crisis, firms tried to outdo each other by attacking the militant craft-protection of the engineers and introducing piecework.[3] The decline in the value of industrial output relative to fixed capital investment revealed "the law of tendency of the falling rate of profit," as later explored by Marx in volume 3 of *Capital*.

When the cotton spinning process had first been mechanized in the late eighteenth century, the male spinners had forced woman out of production. But with the introduction of power-loom weaving in the late 1820s, a huge female workforce entered the mills and by the early 1830s there were more women than men working in textiles. Women came to the forefront in the fight against the Poor Law Amendment Act of 1834. One of the first fruits of the "wedding" between Malthus and Ricardo, this new law was intended to end the old system of parish relief and force the unemployed either into the workhouses or emigration. Women's roles in the past had been restricted to organizing friendly societies (which often financed their husbands' strikes) and Temperance Leagues (which were a means of withholding tax revenue from a corrupt government as well as promoting sobriety among their menfolk). Women often justified their new involvement in politics with the argument that they had "no choice." The new workhouses, nicknamed "Whig Bastilles," represented a deadly threat to their traditional values as home-builders and nurturers.[4]

When William Lovett, leader of the London Working Men's Association, drafted the People's Charter in 1838, he included a clause for the extension of the franchise to women, but this was removed in the face of arguments that it would hold up the enfranchisement of men. Nevertheless, female Chartist organizations sprang up throughout the country in the late 1830s in support of the *male* suffrage and their activity often blended in with the mobilizations against the Poor Law. Women argued that democracy, once established, would need a new generation imbued with democratic ideas by Chartist mothers as well as fathers. To impart such knowledge to their children, women would have to possess it themselves; to get it they would need the same access as men to political education. Although a good number of male Chartists leaders (including George Julian Harney, Bronterre O'Brien, and Henry Vincent, as well as Lovett) favored equal involvement by women in the movement, there was never any serious move to reverse the 1838 decision on female suffrage.

John Foster's *Class Struggle and the Industrial Revolution* describes how in Oldham, Lancashire, the weapon of the "consumer boycott" (largely enforced by women) was used to persuade shopkeepers to elect radical candidates as Poor Law administrators and Police Commissioners (according to a home office spy report, "jacobinical constables" replaced the mill owners' lackeys), as well as to elect John Fielden and William Cobbett as radical M.P.s. As a result, the introduction of the new workhouse system was blocked in the area until the late 1840s, when employment levels rose as the economy recovered.[5] The workers, in fighting the class enemy represented by the mill owners, found common cause with those "democratic elements" of the middle class who were not engaged in textile production. The Oldham phenomenon was not quite a localized "dictatorship of the proletariat," but it did show, in Foster's view, that during the 1830s the "trade union consciousness" of Oldham workers transcended "sectional" interests and developed into a sort of pre-socialist *class* consciousness.

By 1837, George Julian Harney, leader of the London Democratic Association, was touring the North to support an anti–Poor Law campaign and build the Chartist "National Convention." The idea behind the Convention was to elect its "members" at mass popular assemblies so that it could present itself to the people as their legitimate representative body, in direct opposition to the Parliament at Westminster. The mass assemblies were organized and workers in several northern cities began stockpiling pikes and muskets. In February 1839 the Convention went into session in London and a countdown to confrontation with the State began. As Convention delegates debated calling a general strike, the first Chartist petition, with 1,280,000 signatures, was presented to the House of Commons and rejected on July 12 by 235 votes to 46. As a result, street fighting broke out up and down the country and the military commander General Napier began to fear a collapse of authority. This was the closest England came to revolution in the course of the nineteenth century. The Convention collapsed because the "moral force" advocates feared the consequences of the momentum the movement for democracy had built up, but the breakup of the Convention led to the failed insurrections by "physical forcers" at Newport and Sheffield.[6] In the aftermath, Daniel O'Connell, M.P., split the Chartists in 1840 when he led his Manchester Irish contingent into an alliance with the free traders of the Anti–Corn Law League. But the National Charter Association (N.C.A.) resumed the campaign and by 1841 had 350 branches, mostly in the North.[7]

In the summer of 1842, after the House of Commons rejected a Second Chartist Petition, cotton spinners in Lancashire walked out and called for a general strike for the Charter. The strike was named the "Plug Plot" after workers brought production to a halt by pulling the plugs out of factory boilers. As the strike spread out to the Midlands, Wales, Yorkshire, and Scotland, a national Chartist convention assembled in Manchester and, after some hesitation, decided to support the action. Chartist leader Thomas Cooper hoped that the strike might lead to an insurrection, but Feargus O'Connor denounced it in the Chartist *Northern Star* as a plot by the Anti–Corn Law Leaguers. It wasn't, but with a new downturn in the economy the employers were quite happy to take a holiday from paying out wages. The month-long strike ended when troops moved into areas of unrest. Fifteen hundred were arrested and many were imprisoned, transported to Australia, or forced into exile. Harney was tried for conspiracy, but he had told the Manchester conference that the movement simply lacked the means to take on the armed force of the State. He was acquitted after he told the court that the conference had only met after the strikers had declared for the Charter and therefore couldn't have been involved in any "Plug Plot."[8]

The ineffectiveness of the Chartist leadership in the 1842 strike alienated the trade unionists from the N.C.A. campaign. When the economy revived the following year, they found themselves able to win economic gains from the employers without having to consult politicians. In any case, the N.C.A. had shifted its energies to promoting O'Connor's Land Plan: a scheme, financed by seventy thousand subscriptions, to create a sort of Chartist "yeomanry," selected by lottery, on agricultural settlements. O'Connor, as well as being the most popular Chartist leader of all, was also the most inconsistent. At one time the most vociferous opponent of the Anti–Corn Law Leaguers, O'Connor, by the mid-1840s, was in alliance with them against the Tory Protectionists. Increasingly, the younger leaders—notably Harney and Ernst Jones, the lawyer and official poet for the Land scheme—saw the inevitability of failure under O'Connor's leadership.

According to Foster, the history of the Lancashire workers movement from the 1790s to the 1840s does chart the various stages of class consciousness as outlined in *The Communist Manifesto* of 1848. The *Manifesto* states that: "This proletarian class passes through many phases of development, but its struggle with the middle-class dates from its birth."[9] In the nineteenth century, the struggle passes from individual workplaces to "those of an entire trade in a locality against the individuals of the middle-class who directly use them up." In the "Luddite" phase, the workers "attack not only the middle-class system of production; they destroy machinery and foreign commodities which compete with their products; they burn down factories and try to re-attain the position occupied by the producers of the middle ages." In opposition to Old Corruption and the Corn Laws, the bourgeoisie encourage the workers to form "a more compact union," but do so for "their own political ends." At this stage, "the proletarians do not fight their own enemies but their enemies' enemies." But the alliance of worker and factory owner is constantly eroded by the class struggle at the point of production: in due course, "the incessant improvements in machinery make the position of the proletarians more and more uncertain" and collisions "assume more and more the character of collisions between two classes." The trade unions organize strikes and "here and there the struggle takes the form of riots." Eventually, the *Manifesto* contends, with the spread of railways, steamship lines, and other new means of communication, the working class unites, nationally and internationally, as a political party. Although no such unity existed in 1848, many of the most experienced working-class leaders were, as we shall see, trying to forge it.

A "Different History"

Foster's analysis of the politics of class struggle in industrial Lancashire is disputed by Stedman-Jones. In his 1983 essay "The Language of Chartism," which has influenced much of today's postmodernist thinking on early Labour History, Stedman-Jones denies that the failure of Chartism is to be located in the divisions within the movement, or immature class consciousness, or the long boom that began in the late 1840s. Rather, he suggests, the movement's rise and fall should be related in the first instance "to the changing character and policies of the State—the principal enemy upon whose actions radicals had always found that their credibility depended." Chartism, he argues, was limited by a "vocabulary of exclusion" inherited from the radical political discourses of the eighteenth century, which focused on Old Corruption rather than what was capitalistically new. Increasingly, and especially after 1848, when economic growth stabilized, the old and new ruling classes were able to unite around a new reformist consensus of "order" versus "anarchy." Chartism, "as a coherent political language and a believable political vision," really disintegrated in the early 1840s, not the early 1850s. A "class-based language of socialism" only began to emerge much later, in the 1880s. In contrast with "modern socialism," Chartism was based on the precept that the fundamental divisions in society were political rather than economic.[10]

In his critique of Foster, Stedman-Jones writes:

> Undoubtedly, in the last years of Chartism, something like the beginning of modern socialism could be detected. "Chartism in 1850," wrote "Howard Morton" in the first issue of the *Red Republican*, "is a different thing from Chartism in 1840. The leaders of the English proletarians . . . have progressed from the idea of simple political reform to the idea of social revolution." But

by the time the *Red Republican* appeared, the huge hopes and heroic struggles . . . were a thing of the past. The *Red Republican* was the beginning of a different history."[11]

Ironically perhaps, Howard Morton, the *Red Republican* contributor quoted by Stedman-Jones, was in reality Helen Macfarlane, the anonymous translator of *The Communist Manifesto* as serialized in Harney's *Red Republican* in 1850—a fact that no one investigating this "different history" managed to uncover for over a hundred years. (Morton's identity was eventually discovered in 1958 by A. R. Schoyen, a scholar from the United States.) Macfarlane, a supporter of the "Fraternal Democrats" in Lancashire and one of the most prolific of Harney's stable of writers, was forced to adopt a male pseudonym in order to get her writings into print. As we will see, the Fraternal Democrats collaborated with Marx and Engels in a far-sighted attempt, in 1850, to create an international socialist organization, fourteen years before the founding of Marx's First International. But the "different history" Stedman-Jones has in mind is that of "modern socialism," which dates from the growth in the 1880s and 1890s of the "New Model" trade unions and Second International Marxism. In this context it is interesting to compare Stedman-Jones's position, not only with other theorists and historians, but also with one of the participants in this "different history," an "immature" socialist of the 1830s who was still around in the 1890s: George Julian Harney himself, editor of the *Red Republican*. To Harney's mind, "modern socialism" in many ways compared unfavorably with the Red Republicanism of his day. In 1890, his old friend Friedrich Engels witnessed the huge May Day gathering in London and declared, "The grandchildren of the Old Chartists are stepping into the line of battle." And when Keir Hardie and John Burns were elected to Parliament as Labour candidates in 1892, Engels shared his excitement with Harney at the prospect of a mass socialist movement finally emerging in the British Proletariat. But Harney was unimpressed: the trade unionists, he told Engels, were just as "greedy" and "selfish" as the capitalist class; the Labour politicians, by making alliances with the Liberals, were simply repeating the disastrous efforts of his "moderate"

Chartist opponents fifty years earlier. Harney wrote to Engels: "You are the Prince of Optimists. . . . My sight is not so good, nor my hope so sanguine. Least of all have I any belief in the Trades Union chiefs and Labour leaders. To not one of them at present before the public would I give a vote."[12]

Harney's judgment of Chartism's grandchildren soon seemed to be borne out. The emerging Labour leaders placed themselves in the tradition of "constitutional," "moral force" Chartism and were keen to exorcise the spirit of militant internationalism as expressed in the pages of the *Red Republican* and *The Communist Manifesto*.

The "Communist Idea" was, in fact, brought to England in 1836, when one of the Jacobin-inspired working-class leaders, Bronterre O'Brien, translated and published Buonarroti's book on Babeuf's "Conspiracy of Equals." As Marx pointed out, the birth of "Communism" had nothing to do with him or Engels:

> The revolutionary movement that began in 1789 with the *Cercle Social*, which in the middle of its course had as its chief representatives Leclerc and Roux and which was temporarily defeated with Babeuf's conspiracy, brought forth the communist idea that Babeuf's friend Buonarroti reintroduced into France after the Revolution of 1830.[13]

Red Republicanism represented a historical continuity with English Jacobinism as well as with the older "moral economy" of English Dissent (as described in E. P. Thompson's *The Making of the English Working Class*). But it was, I shall argue—drawing on some of Gramsci's ideas in his *State and Civil Society* on Hegel's analysis of the same—the beginning of a different history within a process of *dis*continuity and *differentiation*.

Notes

1. John Foster, *Class Struggle and the Industrial Revolution: Early Industrial Capitalism in Three English Towns* (London: Weidenfeld & Nicolson, 1974).

2. E. P. Thompson, *The Making of the English Working Class* (London: Victor Gollancz, 1963), 854–57. See also Noel Thompson, *The People's Science. The Popular Political Economy of Exploitation and Crisis 1816–34* (Cambridge: Cambridge University Press, 1984).

3. Foster, *Class Struggle*, 21.

4. Malcolm I. Thomis and Jennifer Grimnet, *Women and Social Protest 1800–1850*. (London: Croom Helm, 1982), 65–87.

5. Foster, *Class Struggle*, 57.

6. Christopher Ford, "The London Democratic Association and the National Convention," in *Hobgoblin*, nos. 1 and 2, 1999 and 2000.

7. Donald Read, "Chartism in Manchester," in *Chartist Studies*, ed. Asa Briggs (London: MacMillan, 1967).

8. A. R. Schoyen, *The Chartist Challenge: A Portrait of George Julian Harney* (London: Heinemann, 1958), 115–23.

9. All quotations from *The Communist Manifesto* are from Helen Macfarlane's translation, unless otherwise stated.

10. "The Language of Chartism," in *The Chartist Experience: Studies in Working-Class Radicalism and Culture, 1830–1860*, eds. J. Epstein and D. Thompson (London: MacMillan, 1983). See also Bill Schwartz, "Ancestral Citizens," in *New Formations* 28 (spring 1996).

11. "The Class Struggle and the Industrial Revolution," *New Left Review* 90 (London, 1975).

12. Harney to Engels, July 14, 1892. *Marx-Engels Archives*, International Instituut voor Sociale Geschiedenis (Amsterdam) LIV 237; published in *The Harney Papers*, ed. Frank Gees Black and Renee Metevier Black (Amsterdam: ISH, 1969). See also Peter Cadogan, "Harney and Engels," in *International Review of Social History* X (1965), 66–104.

13. Karl Marx, "The Holy Family," in *Collected Works Volume 4*, Karl Marx and Friedrich Engels (Moscow: Progress Publishers, 1964), 60–61.

3

Hegel's England

Tragedy in the Realm of the Ethical

If "Communism" was rooted in the French Revolution, so also was George Wilhelm Friedrich Hegel's Revolution in Philosophy. Hegel's *Phenomenology of Mind,* completed in 1806, doesn't so much deal with actual events in History carried out by individuals, as the unfolding of the "spirit" of freedom, from Greek antiquity onward: a philosophical "voyage of discovery" through history that is also a "journey of despair." Philosophic consciousness reaches a cataclysmic turning point when Rousseau's concept of the General Will "externalizes" itself in the Revolution under the banner of *Liberté, Egalité, Fraternité* and a new Republic of Virtue is established. When continuing social inequalities and conflicts threaten to undermine the new order, the state's response is to preempt any threat to "unity" by instituting a reign of terror in the interests of "Public Safety": instrumental violence is meted out against anyone even suspected of disloyalty. But this unity of the nation is really only the appearance of unity, because those in charge are really merely a faction and so their claim to represent the General Will is necessarily false. They are overthrown and sent to the guillotine, but those who replace them can fare no better, because they too are a faction, representing only individual wills. With Absolute Freedom having undergone self-transformation into its opposite as Absolute Terror, the Revolution consumes itself; the "World Historic Individual" (Napoleon) takes over and imposes bourgeois institutions and legal forms in "every quarter" of the Continent and beyond—although he will finally demonstrate by his actions "the powerlessness of victory." The Idea then flees "its self-destructive sphere of reality," and Mind takes the philosophic truths gained from its experience into the contemplative sphere of Morality. But here it lacks the "force to externalize itself." It "lives in dread of staining the radiance of its inner being by action and existence" and "perseveres in self-willed impotence" as "a sorrow-laden 'Beautiful Soul.'"[1]

The French experience was not, however, the end of the story. Hegel credited the French Enlightenment of the eighteenth century for having "perceived that Nature—the World—must be the embodiment of Reason." But, as the Hegel scholar Joachim Ritter points out, while the French made "deductive positings of new political forms from principles," it was the English and Scottish political economists who provided "the inductive (hermeneutical) theory of the already existing, historically constituted social reality." Hegel regarded Adam Smith as worthy of comparison with Kepler: Smith had grasped that the economy, like the planetary system, "displays to the eye only irregular movements though its laws may none the less be ascertained."[2]

In Hegel's early writings prior to the *Phenomenology*, capitalism is seen as a collision of the bourgeois spirit with itself: a "tragedy in the realm of the ethical"; a dichotomy in which cultural and national "traditions," as well as notions of Citizen, Church, and State, all come face-to-face with a "lower world" of economic "nature," which now invokes its laws against them. The bourgeois Enlightenment, in Hegel's words, had developed a "bestial contempt for all higher values"; under its sway the "divine of tradition," alienated from its historical reality, was being tossed into the world of "superstition" and "entertainment," the temple reduced to "logs and stones" and "the sacred grove to mere timber." With the social division of labor, great wealth had become "indissolubly connected with the direst poverty." In the "worst form of barbarism," all that was fulfilling and "noble" in labor was being reduced to the purely quantitative concepts of a society of "abstract labour."[3] The young Hegel, who would never again look so closely at the position of the laboring classes, anticipates the young Marx. In the words of *The Communist Manifesto*:

> As soon as the bourgeoisie got the upper hand, they destroyed all feudal, patriarchal, idyllic relationships of men. They relentlessly tore asunder the many-sided links of that feudal chain which bound men to their "natural superiors," and they left no bond of union between man and man, save that of bare self-interest, of cash payments. They changed personal dignity into market value, and substituted the single unprincipled freedom of trade for the numerous, hardly earned, chartered liberties of the Middle Ages. Chivalrous enthusiasm, the emotions of piety, vanished before the icy breath of their selfish calculations.

Hegel's later writings attempt, as Ritter puts it, "a positive interpretation of the dichotomy" in bourgeois society and "the objectivity driving it forward"; the "nature principle of society taken over from political economy is understood at the same time as the historical principle of society's emancipatory constitution."[4] Hegel recognized that the true historical content of his epoch had been the French Revolution rather than the postwar Restoration; that the real legacy of the Revolution had been the establishment of those "subjective freedoms"—especially the rights of property—that were conducive to commodity exchange in a civil society of Labour. The English political economist, David Ricardo, had argued that there could be no solutions to social problems except through the untramelled "progress" of economic development. As Marx would later point out, Ricardo was such an "objective" social scientist that he didn't care which classes Capital "slayed" in the process. For Hegel, however, civil society—consisting of manufacturing, commerce, and agriculture, plus the judiciary and public works needed for it to function properly—was a "community of needs" that could not be left to the mercy of economic "laws." As Richard Winfield puts it, Hegel "radically demarcates civil society from the state and conceives both as structures of interaction independent of natural determination, what he develops is not a political, but a thoroughly social economy."[5]

In Hegel's view, the urgent task for the generation whose world had been turned upside down by the Revolution was to establish mediating social structures capable of stabilizing society for future development. His *Philosophy of Right* envisions a legislature for the Prussian state made up of a monarchy reduced to a mere ceremonial function; the Estates of the nobility, burghers, and peasantry; and a state bureaucracy playing an active and educative role as the "Universal Class." But in 1830, Hegel's hopes that the more "realistic" regimes of Restorationist Europe would oversee the needed changes were upset by the July Revolution in France against the reactionary Bourbon monarchy. Hegel summed up the brief history of the French Restoration as a "fifteen-year farce," riven with "mistrust": between a Catholic establishment determined to destroy "as a matter of conscience" all of the new liberties and institutions that had survived the rise and fall of Napoleon, and a bourgeois liberalism equally determined to preserve and extend them. While Hegel recognized that the Old Order was doomed, he was convinced that liberalism, because it appealed only to abstract principles of freedom from the standpoint of the particular, would come into conflict with the universality of the Ethical State. Hegel feared that should the concept of constitutional monarchy fail to take root then there would no longer exist any "higher power" between the interest of feudal privilege and "the demand for more real freedom." The democratic reformers might then, wittingly or not, unleash popular revolt as the agent of transition.

Hegel had hoped that Protestant nations might avoid a violent rupture with the feudal past because the Reformation—Luther's "Revolution of the Spirit"—had established human freedom as "natural destiny." However, when, in England in 1831, the Duke of Wellington's government was defeated in Parliament as a result of the Parliamentary Reform Bill agitation, it became apparent to Hegel that Protestant constitutional monarchies were also vulnerable to revolutionary upheaval. He now realized that his political program for the "backward" states of Germany had little relevance to any industrialized nation. The problem in England was that there was no real separation between civil society and the state; what existed there in 1831 was, in the proper sense, hardly a "state" at all. Rather, it was a "state *external*," (emphasis mine) whose function was to protect the wealthy landowners and capitalists from the dispossessed majority who were represented by "the democratic element." In stark contrast with France, Hegel points out, in England the "moment of transition from feudal tenure to property" had "slipped by without giving the farmer class the chance to own land." The Reform Bill was a "hotchpotch" that left intact a fatal "internal contradiction" between the old feudal rights and the "abstract and theoretical principle" that had inflamed Europe in 1789. Hegel did, however, foresee that the Reform Bill would, along with other reforms affecting property, commerce, and freedom of religion, give more power to a "new class" of people: those based in smaller-scale commerce, and manufacturing, the educational and legal professions, the artisan trades, and shop keeping. People from these aspiring middle ranks of society clearly found the existing state of rights "oppressive" and looked for a new "universality"; Hegel adds (rather "provocatively," as David MacGregor notes) that in France the democratic element had "found compensation" for their exclusion from public affairs by taking part in "insurrections, clubs, associations etc."[6]

The great Italian Marxist, Antonio Gramsci, in his *Prison Notebooks*, argues that the functioning of Hegel's state cannot be seen as limited to education, public administration, and policing: "In reality, a multitude of other so-called private initiatives and activities tend to the same end—initiatives and activities which form the apparatus of the political and cultural hegemony of the ruling classes." Gramsci notes the importance Hegel gives to parties and associations which, as "the 'private' woof of the State," organize and educate opinion, and guard against the "vagueness" of consent that is "expressed in the instant of elections."[7] In Hegel's *Philosophy of Right*, this "private" aspect appears in the somewhat feeble form of the "corporation," which is rooted in the old guild system as much as it prefigures the idea of twentieth-century corporatism. In defense of individual rights, the role of the corporation within the ethical state is to provide a mutuality of "recognition" for traders, producers, and consumers. Hegel is, however, rather vague about just what this recognition really amounts to. Herbert Marcuse contends that in Hegel's corporation: "Actually it is not the individual but the economic process that does the recognizing. The individual, therefore, obtains only an ideological good; his compensation is the 'honor' of belonging to the corporation."[8] According to Gramsci, "Hegel's conception belongs to a period in which the spreading development of the bourgeoisie could seem limitless, so that its ethicity and universality could be asserted." But even in Hegel's own lifetime, this assertion was beginning to be contested. As Gramsci points out, the newspapers, clubs, and corresponding societies of the French Revolution that re-emerged in the 1820s underwent a process of "differentiation" and crystallized as new political formations, led by "some highly-developed specimens in Blanqui and Filippo Buonarroti." There is no evidence that Hegel read Buonarroti's book on Gracchus Babeuf's proletarian "Conspiracy of Equals" of 1797 after it was published in France in 1828, or that he had any inkling of the enormous influence it would have. Likewise, although Hegel knew and read the *Globe* newspaper published in Paris, which was staffed by intellectuals influenced by the utopian socialism of Saint-Simon, he would not have been aware of a defining moment of "differentiation" that occurred in the paper's offices during the 1830 Revolution:

> Entering the office of the *Globe*, . . . Blanqui saw editors and contributors walking about the room aimlessly "like souls in an abandoned cloister." . . . They who but a few hours before had made the room vibrate with their self-assurance, looked like a flat tyre. They were a pathetic contrast to the men he had just seen on the barricades. As if to dispel some of the gloom, he spoke loud enough for everyone to hear: "Before the week is over, it will all be settled by rifle shots." All eyes turned to him. . . . The forecast seemed to have ruffled feelings. The philosopher, Theodore Jeffroy, rising to full academic posture

and throwing his head back the better to see the modern Cassandra, replied with disdain: "There will not be any rifle shots." A few hours later, Paris was a battlefield.[9]

Hegel, just before his death in 1831, looked in horror at the prospect of any historical role being played by the "rabble"—by which he meant greedy capitalists and useless fox-hunting aristocrats as well as rebellious workers. The problem in England was:

> An opposition building itself on a program hitherto foreign to Parliament and feeling itself unable to expand its influence among the other parties in Parliament might be induced to seek its strength among the people; then instead of achieving a reform it would bring forth a revolution.

Left Hegelians

According to Stedman-Jones, the young Marx of 1844 extends Feuerbach's antireligious critique of Hegel in a way that implies the "recuperation" by consciousness of an "alienated essence." He claims that for Marx, as for Hegel, consciousness is seen as an "a-historical subject" and that both Hegel and Marx make an "ontological" appeal "to a moment of absolute truth, to which no concrete historical process could ever aspire."[10] It is true that Marx, in his 1841 doctoral thesis on the *Difference between the Democritean and Epicurean Philosophies of Nature*, projects a concept of *praxis*, in which the "liberated" theoretical mind presents a *"critique* that measures the individual existence by the *essence,* [and] the particular reality by the *Idea*"[11] (emphases mine). At this early stage in Marx's development, the "energizing principle" of the subject is unformulated. Within a year or so, however, the struggles of the poor begin to feature in his journalism for the *Rheinische Zeitung* and in 1843 Engels sends him enthusiastic reports on the class struggles in England, which at the same time criticize the English socialists for their lack of any philosophical grasp of "the threads of historical progress." Engels also sends

Marx his *Outlines of a Critique of Political Economy,* which has a decisive influence on Marx's thinking:

> Political economy came into being as a natural result of the expansion of trade, and with its appearance elementary, unscientific huckstering was replaced by a developed system of licensed fraud or science of enrichment . . . born of the merchants' mutual envy and greed, [it] bears on its brow the most detestable selfishness.[12]

Hegel, in his *Philosophy of Right,* argues that although it is necessary for civil society to assign (or consign) individuals to their allotted places through "class divisions," the relations between those involved in production and exchange must be "reciprocal" and made universal though a "system of needs":

> Each man in earning, producing, and enjoying on his own account is *eo ipso* producing and earning for the enjoyment of everyone else. The *compulsion* that brings this about is rooted in the *complex interdependence* of *each* on *all,* and it now presents itself to *each* as the *universal permanent capital.*[13] [emphasis mine]

In 1843 Marx criticizes Hegel for philosophizing from the standpoint of "modern political economy" and failing to see that "the principle underlaying civil society is neither need, natural moments, nor politics. It is fluid division of masses whose various formations are arbitrary and *without* organization." At this point, the Proletariat makes its appearance:

> The class of immediate labour, of concrete labour, do not so much constitute a class of civil society as provide the ground on which the circles of civil society move and have their being. . . . The present state of society is distinguished from that which preceded it by the fact that civil society does not sustain the individual as a member of a community, as a communal being (*Gemeinwessen*).[14]

In his 1844 *Critique of the Hegelian Dialectic,* Marx writes that the "greatness" of Hegel's "dialectic of negativity as the moving and creative principle" is its grasp of the "essence of labour" and

the possibility of human self-realization through human collec-
tivity and "as a result of history."[15] As mediation between subject and object, Hegel poses Activity but presents it only as
thinking activity mediating between thought-entities. Marx, in
contrast (and contrary to Stedman-Jones's interpretation), does
not project the notion of an alienated human essence unconditioned by history and mediated only by thought categories. As
he puts it in the *Sixth Theses on Feuerbach* in 1845:

> Feuerbach resolves the religious essence into the human
> essence. But the human essence is no abstraction in each single
> individual. In its reality it is the ensemble of the social relations.

Helen Macfarlane's observation that between 1840 and 1850
"The leaders of the English proletarians . . . [had] progressed
from the idea of simple political reform to the idea of social revolution," is a projection of what George Lichtheim describes as
the "originality" insight of Marx in 1843–1844:

> The belief that a mere spark of critical self-awareness could ig-
> nite a revolutionary tinder heaped up by the inhuman condi-
> tions of life imposed on the early proletariat. In enabling the
> oppressed to attain an adequate consciousness of their true
> role, critical theory translates itself into revolutionary practice.

Consciousness was able to grasp "the total historical situation in which it is embedded . . . because at certain privileged
moments a 'revolution in thought' acquired the character of a
material force."[16]

In Macfarlane's words in 1850:

> As Hegel expresses it, "Freedom is a necessary conception in the
> concept, man." The German thinkers, from Kant to Hegel, were
> the apostles and pioneers of the democratic movement, at pres-
> ent shaking society to its foundation, throughout the German
> empire. The next step in the history of this idea, will be its prac-
> tical realization—that is, the reconstruction of society in accor-
> dance with the democratic idea. Is it for a moment to be
> supposed that this idea—having, despite all opposition, passed

through so many phases, or moments of its development—will stop short of the next and final one?[17]

Joseph Schumpeter describes *The Communist Manifesto* as representing the "transformation of historic narrative into historic reason"; the projection of a historic drama, whose completion the reader was invited to participate in. Helen Macfarlane was one of the first to accept the invitation.

Notes

1. G. W. F. Hegel, *Phenomenology of Mind,* trans. J. B. Baillie (New York: Harper Torchbooks, 1967), 600–667.

2. Joachim Ritter, *Hegel and the French Revolution* (Cambridge: MIT Press, 1982), 69.

3. See George Lukacs, *The Young Hegel* (London: Merlin, 1975), 43–56 and 398–420.

4. Ritter, *Hegel,* 74–83.

5. Richard Dien Winfield, introduction to Ritter, *Hegel.*

6. G. W. F. Hegel, "The English Reform Bill," in *Political Writings,* ed. Z. Pelczynski (Oxford: Oxford University Press, 1964), 295–333. David MacGregor, *Hegel, Marx, and the English State* (Boulder, Colo.: Westview Press, 1992), chap. 1.

7. Antonio Gramsci, "The State and Civil Society," *Selections from the Prison Notebooks* (London: Lawrence and Wishart, 1971), 259–60.

8. Herbert Marcuse, *Reason and Revolution* (Boston: Beacon Press, 1960), 212–13.

9. Samuel Bernstein, *Auguste Blanqui* (London: Lawrence and Wishart, 1971), 33–34.

10. Gareth Stedman-Jones, "The Class Struggle and the Industrial Revolution," *New Left Review* 90.

11. Karl Marx and Friedrich Engels, *Collected Works Vol. 1* (New York: International Publishers, 1975), 85.

12. Marx and Engels, *Collected Works Vol. 3,* 418.

13. G. W. F. Hegel, *Philosophy of Right* (Oxford: Oxford University Press, 1967) 99.

14. Karl Marx, *Early Writings* (London: Pelican, 1975), 147–48.

15. Marx, *Early Writings,* 386.

16. George Lichtheim, *Lukacs* (London: Fontana, 1971), 64–65.

17. Helen Macfarlane, "Democracy," *Democratic Review,* June 1850.

4

Fraternal Democrats

The First Internationalists

George Julian Harney, by the time he was twenty years of age in 1837, had served three prison sentences for selling "unstamped" newspapers. Universally despised as the "knowledge tax," the Stamp Duty had been imposed by the government in order to put the price of news and political analysis beyond the pockets of working people. Young Harney first learned his politics from Jacobin veterans of the London Corresponding Society who had been active back in the 1790s. His development as a socialist was influenced by Thomas Spence, Robert Owen, and Bronterre O'Brien, as well as the American Fourierists, whose writings from the *New York Tribune* and *Working Man's Advocate* crossed the Atlantic to the pages of the Feargus O'Connor's *Northern Star* in Leeds.

In 1838, Harney found himself in the leadership of a movement that seemed to be moving toward an insurrectionary showdown with the State. In the early 1840s, following the breakup of the Chartist National Convention, Harney became one of the most popular and widely heard lecturers of the National Charter Association and joined the editorial staff of O'Connor's *Northern Star*. In this latter role he met Friedrich Engels, who was researching his book *The Condition of the English Working Class*. At

Harney's suggestion, Engels wrote an analysis of "Continental Socialism" for the *Star* in 1843 and for a time became the paper's Paris correspondent.[1]

By 1845, the circulation of the *Star* had declined from its 1839 peak of forty thousand copies weekly to ten thousand. In a move to bolster circulation, O'Connor moved its office to London and appointed Harney as editor at the new premises in Great Windmill Street. Harney immediately threw the paper's columns open to the German, Polish, Italian, and French revolutionaries of the London *émigré* community who had congregated in Soho. Although the various nationalities regularly came together for each other's anniversary celebrations, there was no permanent body of international solidarity, so Harney decided to try and unite the various groups on a political basis. In this he found a key ally in Karl Schapper, a German artisan who had led a conspiratorial group in Paris known as the League of the Just, later renamed the Communist League. Schapper and other League members had fled to London in 1839 after participating in a failed insurrection in Paris led by Auguste Blanqui. In London the German Communists were building Workers Educational Societies among the German refugees.

Harney's efforts in international solidarity were set against three rival currents of "foreign policy." At the top there were the diplomatic and military initiatives of the Foreign Office to strengthen Britain's European alliances and provide assistance to allies whenever they were threatened by revolt. Thus Hapsburg Austria, for example, was given a free hand to join forces with Russia to invade Polish territory whenever democracy or nationalism reared its head. Secondly, there were the Manchester Liberals, who called for financial sanctions against "protectionist Austria" so as to help liberate her subject nationalities, such as the Poles and Hungarians, as "free-trading peoples." Thirdly, there was the internationalism of the Chartist "moderate," William Lovett, who launched a body called the "Democratic Friends of All Nations" in early 1845. But when Lovett published its first address, which condemned armed struggle even against the most tyrannical regimes, the emigrés—mostly Poles—pulled out and the organization collapsed.[2] It was at this point that a triumvirate comprising Schapper, Harney, and Ernst Jones moved to found a new international organization with a distinctly working-class and democratic perspective. Named the Society of Fraternal Democrats, it was built up in a semi-clandestine fashion in late 1845 and early 1846. Many of those involved in setting it up had, like Harney, been members of the London Democratic Association (L.D.A.) in the 1830s. The plan for a new organization seems to have been hatched at an L.D.A. anniversary dinner, held on August 11, 1845, at the Angel Inn, Blackfriars Road. The "Babeufian" socialist language of the founding statements of the Fraternal Democrats is virtually identical to statements of the L.D.A.[3]

Initially the society had no officers or rules. There were no subscription payments because it was thought money would only be needed for specific purposes and could be raised by voluntary contributions, with each contributing according to their means.[4] In March 1846, the names of the society's members were enrolled as a preventative measure against potential disrupters and spies; six language secretaries (in English, German, French, Slavonic, Scandinavian, and Swiss) were appointed "for the purpose of authenticating all documents issued to the public." It was argued that no other officers were needed since it was not "a society or party, but merely an assemblage of men belonging to different countries . . . [for] the purpose of mutual information." At an international rally for the new organization, Harney denounced the chauvinism and xenophobia that was all too often manifested in the speeches of English radicals, such as Cobbett and O'Connor. To great cheers Harney declared: "We repudiate the word 'foreigner'—it shall not exist in our democratic vocabulary." At the founding banquet of the Democrats even the Moslem world was represented by a "Democratic Turk," who entertained them with music.[5]

The founding of the Fraternal Democrats posed in a new way the problem of how a small organization of activists relates to the broader popular movement. Harney, writing to Engels in March 1846, confides: "We were for some time regarded with much prejudice and jealousy by the Chartists, but this is wearing away." Members of the Chartist executive had visited Harney when they learned of the new organization and expressed fears that the Fraternal Democrats "would take the popular leadership out of their hands," but Harney had replied: "You lead, we will follow. Our policy is not to push ourselves, but our principles, and compel others to adopt them." Ernst Jones wrote: "There was at its formation a slight distrust on the part of my Chartist brethren against the Fraternal Democrats—they feared it was an attempt to supersede the movement—to create a party within a party; they have now learned that every member of this society is a thorough Chartist, and that Chartism is a test of admission for its members."[6]

In spring 1846 Harney co-opted the Chartist executive to join with the London Poles in celebration of the Krakow Uprising. The revolutionary government of Krakow, led by John Tyssowski, had issued a social-democratic manifesto, calling for "a state of society in which every man shall enjoy his share of the fruits of the earth according to his merits and his capacity . . . every man disabled by nature in the use of his bodily or mental functions will receive without humiliation the unfailing assistance of the whole social state."[7] But the Republic was crushed within weeks by the armed forces of Russia and Austria. When Krakow was annexed by Austria, in clear violation of the Treaty of Vienna, the Fraternal Democrats called for British military intervention to restore Krakow's sovereignty. Later, in 1849, the Democrats were to call for armed intervention to save Hungary from the armies of Russia and Austria. However, as a general rule, they opposed the British government's own military initiatives: when, in 1846, a dispute between Britain and the United States over the possession of Oregon threatened to develop into a war, the Democrats issued an address to the workers of both countries saying a war "would distract public attention from your grievances . . . and would postpone your political emancipation. . . . There is no foot of land in Britain or the colonies, that you, the working-class, can call your own. . . . They, your masters, will take the land . . . of the new colonies . . . your share will be the slaughter of the combat." A follow-up address took the opportunity of protesting against U.S. incursions into Mexico on behalf of the slave owners.[8]

On the first anniversary of the founding of the Fraternal Democrats on September 21, 1846, Harney outlined the organization's program, which was adopted in full:

> We renounce, repudiate, and condemn all hereditary inequalities and distinctions of caste; we declare that the earth with all its natural productions is the common property of all; we declare that the present state of society which permits idlers and schemers to monopolise the fruits of the earth, and the productions of industry, and compels the working-class to labour for inadequate rewards, and even condemns them to social slavery, destitution and degradation, is essentially unjust."[9]

In the 1847 General Election, Harney caused a sensation when he stood against Foreign Secretary Palmerston in Tiverton and engaged him at the hustings in a lively debate about foreign policy, covering everything from the government's collaboration with European despots to its forcing of the opium trade on China. Harney won the vote by a show of hands and Palmerston then had to call for a poll of the men of property in order to take the seat.

In July 1847 the Fraternal Democrats adopted a firmer organizational structure by introducing a membership fee of one shilling a year and electing a central committee. This consisted of general secretaries representing the British, German, French, Scandinavian, Swiss, Polish, and Hungarian nationalities, plus five Chartists, including Ernst Jones, Thomas Clark, and Philip McGrath. In November 1847 a London meeting of the Fraternal Democrats to commemorate the 1830 Polish Uprising was attended by Marx, representing the Brussels-based *Association Démocratique*. By this time the Manchester Liberal "internationalists" had regrouped as the People's International League with the support of Mazzini, leader of the antisocialist Italian republicans, and Czartoryski, the aristocratic leader of the Society of Polish Emigrants, and had organized an international congress in Brussels to promote pacifism and free trade. Marx, in his speech to the London meeting, called for an international congress of workers at Brussels, scheduled for September 25,

1848. The Chartists, he said, were the "real democrats" of England, and if successful, they would be "hailed as the saviours of the whole human race." The Fraternal Democrats subsequently debated Marx's proposal and unanimously decided to use their influence on the N.C.A. executive to get the British Chartist movement to support the congress and convene a second one in London in September 1849.[10] No doubt Marx, as he prepared *The Communist Manifesto* for the printer at the end of 1847, was looking forward to the exciting possibility that the English Chartists might take the lead in proposing its principles as the basis for an international workers party. Owing to unforeseen circumstances, however, the congress never took place.

Chartism in 1848

The newsboards at Charing Cross Station announcing the February Revolution in France sent Harney running through Soho "like a bedlamite" to tell Schapper and the other exiles. The revolutionaries returned to their homelands to put their ideas to the test. Harney, Jones, and McGrath traveled to Paris as guests of the revolutionary government at the Tuileries. Harney playfully sat on the emptied throne of Louis Philippe, and looked forward to performing a similar ceremony at Buckingham Palace. When the Chartists called for a mass mobilization at Kennington Common on April 10, 1848, to march on Parliament with the Third Petition for the Charter, the government, with wary eyes on events in France, met the challenge as an emergency and organized the middle classes en masse as special constables. Prime Minister Lord John Russell wrote to Albert, the Queen's Consort, on the day before the march, regarding the military mobilization, "I have no doubt of their easy triumph over a London mob. But any loss of life will cause a deep and rankling resentment. I trust, for this and every reason, that all may pass off quietly."[11]

With perhaps one hundred thousand marchers assembling, O'Connor gave in to police threats to prevent the marchers crossing the river to Westminster, though he was allowed to send a carriage to deliver the petition. Torrential rain helped to ensure an orderly retreat and dispersal amid angry shouts of "No More Petitions!" at O'Connor, whose deals with the reforming liberals had failed to achieve anything. Some physical-force Chartists regrouped with the Irish radicals and began to make plans for insurrection. Units of a "National Guard" were formed by Chartists in several Northern towns and in London, Chartists began drilling on the streets of Clerkenwell. Uprisings broke out in the North, but were quickly put down by troops and police, as was an attempt to organize a peasant uprising in Ireland. Jones fell victim to a new Crown and Government Security Act when he was arrested for making "seditious" speeches in June 1848 and sentenced to two years imprisonment. In August a group of London Chartists tried to organize an uprising, but the leaders were arrested after a police raid on the Orange Tree pub in Seven Dials. This plot, organized along Blanquist lines, had been "ripened" by government spies and provocateurs who planted arms at meeting places. One of those hauled in as a leader of the conspiracy was the tailor, William Cuffay. An executive member of the National Charter Association, Cuffay was the son of a black slave and a white woman, born in 1788 on a ship en route from St. Kitts to Chatham. Cuffay was the first political activist in Britain to be subjected to the poison of anti-black racism in the press. (The *Times*, in reporting his trial, which ended with his deportation to Australia for life, referred to the Chartists as "the black man's party.")[12]

The government spying system then in operation was much less formalized than it later became with the founding of the Scotland Yard Special Branch in 1883. In 1848, the Home Office got its secret reports from magistrates who employed spies, and from the Lord Lieutenants of the counties who coordinated intelligence from soldiers sent to gather information in public houses. The government could also count on help from local postmasters, factory inspectors and journalists (gentlemen of the press who made verbatim reports of political meetings frequently appeared in political trials as witnesses for the prosecution).[13]

The Fraternal Democrats' formal relationship with European revolutionaries was circumscribed from May 1848 by the British government's new Aliens Act, which gave the Home Secretary increased powers to order deportations of "foreign troublemakers." As a result, the Fraternal Democrats absolved all of the foreign members of its central committee from duties and activities so as to immunize them from deportation. Forty years after the event, Harney wrote that, compared with the days of the Chartist Convention in 1838 and 1839, when the masses had been energized and insurrection was "in the air," Kennington in 1848 was a "fiasco."[14]

Before 1848, Jones had been one of the leaders who, along with O'Connor, had urged the movement not to break from its alliances with the middle-class parties; but when Jones came out of prison in 1850 he declared himself a "Communist" and a sworn opponent of the bourgeoisie. Jones recalled in 1852 that in 1848 all "had been all fire and impulse for two months of the spring," as "one shot of triumphant resolution after another came pealing from the continent" to inspire the peoples' struggle against their "trembling opponents." But

> just at that time they were too apathetic to leave their own doors and walk half a mile for a meeting. It is no excuse to say "they had no confidence in their leaders." . . . Had they confidence in *themselves* they would not have cared about their leaders! But worse than this, the popular straw had burnt out for the time being—the people were too *lazy* to be democratic.[15] [emphasis original]

Breaking with the Bourgeoisie

Both Jones and Harney highlighted the movement's lack of effectiveness in two key areas: organization and "social propaganda." As an organizational initiative within Chartism, the Fraternal Democrats, along with O'Brien's Reform League, declared working-class independence from those still tied to the Manchester Liberals and the ex–Corn Law Repealers. In changing the green flag for the red, a break with O'Connor became inevitable. Whereas in the 1842 General Strike, O'Connor had told the trade unionists and cooperators that only a "political" campaign focused on the Charter could bring about change, in 1848 he backed away from the political struggle to give even greater priority to the Chartist Land Plan. But O'Connor's back-to-the-land dream was facing financial collapse. O'Brien argued that even if the Plan ever succeeded it would merely strengthen the forces of reaction; Harney, as a "Spencean" socialist on the Land Question, had always argued for wholesale nationalization of the land as the "Peoples Farm." The differences with O'Connor on Land paralleled a divide in the German Communist League between William Weitling's idea of a communism of petty producers and smallholding farmers and the proletarian orientation of Schapper and Marx.

By 1848, the expansion of railways and telegraphy, along with developments in printing technology, had brought about a national mass media in Britain, thus giving working-class people increased access to news of events and political ideas. But the Chartist press was not in good shape following the setbacks of 1848. By spring 1849, O'Connor's *Northern Star* was floundering in the midst of a heated debate in its columns between O'Connor and Harney, this time on "Foreign Policy." O'Connor accused his upstart editor in chief of alienating middle-class opinion by promoting "excessive" republicanism and "meddling" in foreign affairs. Meanwhile, Harney pointed out that it was Feargus himself who had pioneered the republican slant and internationalist coverage, and that many readers took the paper because of the reliability of its "Foreign Intelligence" columns. Furthermore, as Rothstein observes, to frighten workers by the prospect of desertion by bourgeois "friends" was "altogether comical" to Harney and Jones after the betrayals of April 1848 in England and the bourgeois terrorism of the June Days in France.[16]

When O'Connor began negotiating a "Charter-by-installments" deal with the Liberals, and his Land Plan administrator Thomas Clark declared Chartism as "finished," the Fraternal Democrats mobilized the Chartist rank and file against them. By early 1850, the Fraternal Democrats had gained a majority on the executive of the National Charter Association and had twenty of their own Fraternal Democrat chapters "stretching from Aberdeen to Plymouth," dedicated to political education and "social propaganda." As Schoyen points out, "their potentiality as propagators of the new movement was not proportionate to their numbers. Such activists had always become leaders when the working-class threw up their mass-movements."[17] The question was whether or not the "social propaganda" of the revolutionaries could relate to the existing working-class movements, such as the cooperatives and trade unions. Harney believed that the new Fraternal Democrat presses—the monthly *Democratic Review* and the weekly *Red Republican*—could do just that.

Notes

1. Schoyen, *Chartist Challenge*, 201.

2. Mary Davis, "The Forerunners of the First International: The Fraternal Democrats," *Marxism Today*, February 1971.

3. Christopher Ford, *Hobgoblin*, nos. 1 and 2, 1999 and 2000.

4. Harry Weisser, *British Working-Class Movements and Europe 1815–48* (Manchester: Manchester University Press, 1975), 137.

5. Theodore Rothstein, *From Chartism to Labourism* (London: Lawrence and Wishart, 1983), 129.

6. *Northern Star*, February 5, 1848; Rothstein, *From Chartism*, 129.

7. Weisser, *British Working-Class*, 143.

8. Weisser, *British Working-Class* 38.

9. *Principles and Rules, Adopted by the Fraternal Democrats*, British Museum Cataloque 1857-e-4(33).

10. Weisser, *British Working-Class* 143; Marx and Engels, *Collected Works Vol. 6*, 616.

11. Quoted in F. C. Mather, *Public Order in the Age of the Chartists* (Manchester: Manchester University Press, 1959).

12. Ron Ramdin, *The Making of the Black Working-Class in Britain* (London: Gower, 1987), 25–28. Schoyen, *Chartist Challenge*, 206.

13. Tony Bunyan, *History and Practice of the Political Police in Britain* (London: Quartet, 1983).

14. G. J. Harney, "The Tremendous Uprising, in 3 Parts," *Newcastle Weekly Chronicle*, December 27, 1888 to January 30, 1889.

15. *Notes to the People, May 1851–May 1852*; ed. by Ernest Jones (London: Merlin Press, 1967), 279.

16. Rothstein, *From Chartism to Labourism*, 148.

17. Schoyen, *Chartist Challenge*, 201.

5

The Mystery of a Nom de Plume

The weekly *Red Republican* was launched by George Julian Harney in June 1850. Harney placed great importance on coverage of international politics and there were now in London more exiled revolutionaries from Germany, France, Poland, Hungary, and France than ever to contribute their writings to his weekly and his monthly *Democratic Review*. Domestic coverage in the *Red* would feature reports on the struggles of type-founders, power-loom weavers, engine drivers, miners, and shoemakers; heated debates between Chartist leaders on whether or not to water down Chartist demands; editorials by Harney; and commentary by writers such as the republican writer W. J. Linton, the poet and essayist Gerald Massey, and Howard Morton.

At this point, the evidence that Howard Morton was indeed Helen Macfarlane—as first claimed by Harney's biographer Schoyen in 1958—must be considered. Macfarlane's role as translator of *The Communist Manifesto* for the *Red Republican* in 1850 wasn't revealed until twenty years later, when Marx and Engels mentioned it in their 1872 introduction to a new German edition. Apart from that, the only work of Macfarlane in her own name consists of a long three-part essay appearing in the April, May, and June 1850 issues of the *Democratic Review* titled *Democracy: Remarks on the Times Apropos of Certain Passages in No. 1 of Thomas Carlyle's "Latter-Day" Pamphlet*. A debut article by

Morton appears in the June 22, 1850, issue of the *Red*; after that, Macfarlane's name disappears from the *Review* and Morton credits begin appearing there. All of Morton's writings have the same unmistakable style as Macfarlane's and show the influence of *The Communist Manifesto*, which had thus far only appeared in German. After Macfarlane's parting from Harney at the end of 1850, there are no more Morton credits in Harney's presses. Schoyen points out that the name Howard Morton does not appear in any known lists of those attending Chartist meetings or in any other surviving documentation—as do all other writers of similar importance. Howard Morton does, however, get a mention in one of the *Red's* "Notices to Correspondents" columns, in which Fraternal Democrat member G. J. Mantle writes from Manchester on the Red Republican "fighting fund":

> I have raised among my friends 10s 6d, as follows—Howard Morton (the *veritable* "Howard Morton") 5s, John Knight 2s 6d. [emphasis original]

It is the aside ("the *veritable*"), which begins to give the game away.

If Morton was in Lancashire and near Manchester, so was Macfarlane. This is revealed in a letter from Harney to Engels, dated December 16, 1850, telling him: "The address of Miss Macfarlane is: Bridgend, Burnley."[1] A letter from London written by Marx's wife, Jenny, to Engels in Manchester on December 19, 1850, encloses a bundle of the *Neue Rheinische Zeitung*, and tells him that Harney "wishes you to send one on to Helen Macfarlane."[2] As Phyliss Bell points out, Mantle was part of a study group in Manchester, organized by Engels, on the ideas of "Continental Socialism."[3] This suggests that the "friends" were members of this semi-clandestine group, which was probably one of the "social propaganda" cells of the Fraternal Democrats. (John Knight was the name of a long-dead cotton spinners' leader once prosecuted for Luddism—Fraternal Democrats often recycled such names as noms de guerre.)

The letter from Harney to Engels on December 1850 that provides Helen Macfarlane's address in Burnley suggests that she had moved there after living in London: most of the articles by Morton that were published earlier in the year concern events taking place in the capital, whereas articles published later in the year—from August onward—tend to cover events in Manchester. The same letter tells Engels, "Don't forget the 'Helen'" when writing to her. This suggests that there were other Macfarlanes living there; and this is confirmed by the 1851 National Census records, taken three and a half months after Harney's letter.[4] Residing at No. 3 Bridgend on the night of March 30, 1851, were William T. Macfarlane, a calico printer, age thirty-three and his sister, Agnes, age fourteen (no occupation). Calico printers were often well-off independent entrepreneurs and it seems that the Macfarlane household was part of a well-off neighborhood, judging by the occupations recorded for other residents of the street and by the fact that the Macfarlanes had a house servant, Elizabeth Thompson, age twenty-two, who is also listed in the Census. Helen, as a "Miss," was presumably William's and Agnes's sister, but she was not staying in the house the night the Census was taken. The Census records that both William and Agnes Macfarlane were born in Scotland. Since Agnes was born there around 1836, when her brother was about twenty years old, this makes it likely that Helen also grew up in Scotland.[5] And since the birthdates of youngest and eldest siblings are not usually more than twenty years apart it is probable that William's date of birth (around 1816) was earlier than hers. We know that Helen was an adult by 1845, because she writes (as Morton): "In 1845, I was informed, by an eminent physician in London that the number of prostitutes there was about eighty thousand. In 1850, I have been told the number is about one hundred thousand"—clearly, for those times, an "adult" conversation.[6]

The debut article by Morton for the *Red* claims that "Chartism in 1850 is a different thing from Chartism in 1840," now that "English proletarians" had "proved they are the true democrats" and "progressed from the idea of simple political reform to the idea of Social Revolution."

"Returning lately to this country after a long absence of some years [emphasis mine], I was agreeably surprised by this fact, 'What old Mole; workest thou in the earth so fast?'"[7]

We know also that Macfarlane had returned to England from abroad because she states, under her own name in the *Democratic Review*, that she had witnessed the 1848 Revolution in Vienna. For Macfarlane, a "joyful spectacle" was enacted when, following the overthrow of Louis Philippe in France in February 1848, the tide of Revolution reached Austria in the space of a few weeks. In March, the citizens of Vienna overthrew the government of Prince Metternich and forced Emperor Ferdinand to concede a representative Diet and a new constitution. But the Hapsburgs played for time and struck back. In October, Field Marshall Windischgratz ordered his artillery to shell the streets of Vienna and then sent his Croatian troops into the city, where they restored the status quo after a bloody three-day battle of the barricades. The new Emperor, Franz Joseph, annulled the constitution.

As to the question of what brought Macfarlane to Vienna in the first place, it is noteworthy that middle-class girls in Macfarlane's time were more likely to be taught modern languages (German and French in her case) than boys, who were usually taught Latin or Ancient Greek in the public schools. Middle-class education for girls was designed to equip young women for employment as teachers or governesses. Macfarlane's proficiency in German and familiarity with literature and history is then, a clue to any employment she might have had in Vienna. Her whereabouts between the Revolution and her appearance in England in early 1850 are not known.

Notes

1. *The Harney Papers*, ed. Frank Gees Black and Renee Metevier Black (Amsterdam: Institute of Social History, 1969), 157.
2. Marx and Engels, *Collected Works Vol. 38*, 560.
3. Phyliss Bell, "Helen Macfarlane, Chartist and Marxist," *Marx Memorial Library Bulletin*, April and June 1975.
4. Public Record Office, *HO 107 2252*.
5. In the Scottish Church Records of births and christenings held at the National Archives of Scotland there are several entries each for

"William," "Helen," and "Agnes" Macfarlane in the relevant respective time spans. But as there is no commonality of father's names and places of birth it is not possible to identify the parentage or place(s) of birth for the three siblings from these records.

6. *Red Republican*, November 11, 1850.
7. *Red Republican*, June, 22 1850.

6

Humbug Manufacturers and Rosewater Sentimentalists

Manchester Men

For the Red Republicans, the most immediate threat to working-class organizational independence and unity came from the Manchester Liberals, who had successfully campaigned against the Corn Laws (repealed by the Peel government in 1846) and hoped to gain further support through an extension of the franchise to a larger section of the middle class. Anti–Corn Law. League founders, Richard Cobden and John Bright, argued that power needed to be transferred from the landed oligarchy to the "intelligent middle and industrious classes." They were, however, supporters of the Malthusian theory that the rate of economic growth would always be outstripped by the rate of population growth and that the high rate of pauperism (one in twelve in England) could only be cured by a reduction in the population. On this basis, they opposed any government intervention aimed at relieving the distress of the poor. "The remedy proposed by this set of quacks," writes Helen Macfarlane in "Labour versus Capital," was emigration.[1] In an article in the *Democratic Review* entitled "Intrigues of the Middle-class Reformers," she writes:

> Messrs. Cobden and Bright, always remind me of that ridiculous couple, Don Quixote and Sancho Panza. There is a mental

hardness about the one, comparable to nothing in the universe, save the physique of the skinny, lanthorn-jawed Don; and about the other—an obtuse, bull-headed dogmatism, a happy self-complacency, very like Sancho in Barataria, laying down the law about everything and everybody, though unable to see one inch, in any direction, beyond the tip of his snub nose. Pity those financial gentlemen had not shared honest Sancho's predilection for the homely wisdom of proverbs. . . . "Show me your companions, and I will tell you what you are."[2]

These companions, Macfarlane points out, included former Chartist leaders, such as Thomas Clark, who were attempting to set up a rival organization with Liberal support. Following the failure of the Kennington Common mobilization of 1848, the Cobden–Bright Liberals had urged moderate Chartist supporters to curtail the six-point People's Charter and join the campaign for a modest extension of the franchise. This drew the comment from Macfarlane that "without the proletarians to back him up, how can Mr. Cobden get up the 'storm of agitation' he promised us? 'superior pyrotechny this evening!'—only the fireworks are not forthcoming."[3] In foreign affairs, the Cobden–Bright radicals argued that Free Trade would bring about international peace between nations as well as domestic peace within nations. In 1850, they helped organize an International Peace Congress at Frankfurt, attended by Liberals, Quakers, and Christian Socialists. Cobden equated freedom with "order and tranquility," but this, according to Macfarlane's article on the Peace Congress, was:

A contradiction in terms. As long as Society is divided into classes, so long will the social system be founded on the distinction of a ruling class and a subordinate class. Now if there be a "spirit of order and tranquility pervading" in the oppressed class, it must be a remarkable stupid class indeed. But as far as my researches have extended into universal history, I have never found an instance of an oppressed class being what their rulers would call "orderly and tranquil." Had they been contented with their sad fate they would have deserved it. No, the slaves of all ages, the helots of Sparta, the Roman bondmen, the serfs of the middle ages, the Negro and proletarian slaves of modern times, have amply and energetically protested against that atrocious system of one class using up another; a system which can only be enforced and continue in any country by the unlimited use of the whip and the bayonet.[4]

Dickens's and Lamartine's London

While the Cobden–Bright party was still committed to a form of "class war" against the British aristocracy, there were others who argued that there was no longer any need to fight it, when so much more could be accomplished by charity. Macfarlane's article of July 20, 1850, "Fine Words (Household or Otherwise) Butter No Parsnips," discusses an article in Charles Dickens *Household Words* about "two poor little starving children who stole a loaf of bread, and were sentenced . . . to be whipped for this awful 'crime against society, property, and order.'" Macfarlane says that as an alternative to such punishments, and as a "cure for hunger," these "rosewater political sentimentalists of the Boz school" prescribed transportation to Australia with spelling books provided by charity.[5] To Macfarlane, the very concept of charity was immoral:

> We feel humiliated and pained when a beggar stretches out his hand to us for "charity"—that insult and indignity offered to human nature; that word invented by tyrants and slave drivers— an infamous word, which we desire to see erased from the language of every civilised people.[6]

Dickens, in a "Preliminary Word" to *Household Words: A Weekly Journal*, launched on March 30, 1850, promises his readers: "No mere utilitarian spirit, no iron binding of the mind to grim realities, will give a harsh tone to our *Household Words*," thus showing some awareness of the potential appeal of anti-utilitarian—and radical— competitors:

> Some tillers of the field into which we now come, have been before us, and some are here whose high usefulness we read-

ily acknowledge, and whose company it is an honour to join. But, there are others here—Bastards of the Mountain, draggled fringe on the Red Cap, Panders to the basest passions of the lowest natures—whose existence is a national reproach. And these, we should consider it our highest service to displace.[7]

Macfarlane, taking Dickens's words as a direct provocation, comments:

> We, the English Socialist-democrats, may be "the ragged fringe on the Red Republican cap, the bastard of the Mountain," as the sapient *Mr. Boz* has been pleased to denominate us, but we are something more than *that*. Chartism and Red Republicanism must henceforward be considered as synonymous terms: to judge from the Executive Council lately chosen by the Chartist party. And what is Chartism? Why, I think if the stones of Kersal Moor, and Peep Green, and Kennington Common [places where enormous Chartist mobilizations had taken place] could find a voice, it would appear that Chartism is something very much re-sembling the hope and aspiration of a majority of the working men of England. Chartism under the Red Flag is a vindication of the Claims of Labour; it is the enunciation of the "Gospel of Work"; the assertion, that the fustian jacket and the paper caps are infinitely more honourable emblems than the ermine robe and the coronet. The symbols of the active brain and the cunning hand, of Man's mastery over inanimate Nature, that of Knowl-edge and Power, set forth in the old Oriental myths as being a link in the chain which connects Humanity with Deity—and Elo-him said "Lo! Adam has become like one of us"—the symbols of labour, I say, are incomparably more honourable than the sym-bols of the force and fraud, which during the dark ages laid the foundation for the present power and wealth of aristocrats and hereditary legislators.[8] [emphasis original]

In Macfarlane's eyes, London in 1850 was the city of "thirty thousand women . . . starving at shirtmaking"; of jails and hulks "recruited from the starving ranks of labour"; of "the women in the streets," nine-tenths of whom were "driven to that fearful life by hunger"; of workhouses "filled to overflowing with able-bodied men"; and men working "eighteen hours a day, baking bread in hot, unhealthy places, for a pittance hardly sufficient to keep soul and body together."[9]

Alphonse de Lamartine, French poet, statesman, and moderate republican, saw London differently, reporting in 1850 on the changes he had seen since his previous visits in the 1830s. Macfarlane quotes Lamartine's praise of the "charity" and "public virtue" of the "intelligent aristocracy" of England, which had, he claimed, showered down many "incalculable benefits from above." The clearance of slums in central London had, he claimed, cleansed the streets of "filth, drunkenness and obscenity. . . . one feels in them the vigilance of public morality, and the presence of a police which, if it cannot destroy vice, can at all events keep it at a safe distance from the eyes of the passer-by." With the slums of Westminster replaced by opulent shops and hotels and the economy on an upswing, there was a new "prudence of the liberal opposition" and a "tenderness evinced towards a conciliation of all classes." The only dissenting voices came from "two classes of men, whom nothing ever satisfies, the demagogues and extreme aristocrats . . . clubs of Chartists and diplomatists."

Throughout the 1840s, "Moral England" had been extraordinarily productive in church-building and mass publication of bibles and religious propaganda. In 1850 a meeting was held in London to protest at the proven fact that female binders employed by the Bible Society were so badly paid for their labor that they frequently had to resort to prostitution to make ends meet.[10] Macfarlane pronounces:

> M. de Lamartine's congratulations upon the "vigilance of public morality" are rather premature. In 1845, I was informed, by an eminent physician in London, that the number of prostitutes there was about eighty thousand. In 1850, I have been told the number is about one hundred thousand; to which increase in the victims of class legislation, cheap Bibles, patronised by the saints of moral England, have largely contributed.[11]

Macfarlane's hostility to the Christian religion as propagated by the "saints of moral England" is clear enough here, as elsewhere in her writings. However, according to her own "religious" view, which we turn to next, the churches and sects were not Christian enough.

Notes

1. *Red Republican*, November 11, 1850.
2. *Democratic Review*, June 1850.
3. *Democratic Review*, June 1850.
4. *Red Republican*, September 14, 1850.
5. *Red Republican*, November 2, 1850.
6. *Red Republican*, October 12, 1850.
7. *Household Words: A Weekly Journal Conducted by Charles Dickens* Vol. 1 No. 1, (London 1850).
8. *Red Republican*, July 13, 1850.
9. *Red Republican*, July 13, 1850.
10. *Notes*, 385.
11. *Red Republican*, November 11, 1850.

7

Christianity and Socialism

> Nothing is easier than to give Christian ascetism a
> tinge of socialism. Has not Christianity itself vocifer-
> ated against private property, marriage, and the pow-
> ers that be? Have not charity, and the mendacity of the
> flesh, monastic life, and the supremacy of the Church
> been held up in the place of these things? Sacred So-
> cialism is merely the holy water with which the priest
> besprinkles the impotent wrath of the Aristocracy.
>
> —"Manifesto of the German Communist Party,"
> *Red Republican*, November 1850

Robert Owen, the "utopian" socialist, disappointed his Christian
sympathizers with his 1836 *Book of the New Moral World*. Against
moral prudery, individualism, and the superstition of priestcraft,
Owen argued for free love, collective solidarity, and a rational
social order. The fact was, however, that many Christians were
so appalled by the condition of the industrial masses and the
"absence of morality" in the utilitarianism of Bentham and
Malthus that they found Owen's utopian collectivism quite compelling. Robert Southey, the Poet Laureate, had met Owen in
1816 and hailed his "model factory" at New Lanark as the ful-
fillment of the utopian "Pantisocracy" that he, Coleridge, and
Wordsworth had dreamed of in the 1790s. Coleridge, even

twenty years after throwing away his "child's trumpet of sedition," railed against Malthusian political economy in his 1817 *Lay Sermon Addressed to the Higher Classes of Society*:

> We will be told . . . that the very Evils of this System, even the periodical *crash* itself, are to be regarded but as so much superfluous steam ejected by the Escape Pipes and Safety Valves of a self-regulating machine: and lastly, that in a free and trading country *all things find their level*. . . . But persons are not *Things* . . . Neither in Body nor in Soul does the man find his level![1] [emphasis original]

Coleridge and Southey, in calling for a new unity of church and state to bring about an "organic Christian society" through the moral conversion of humanity, thus helped to lay the foundations of Christian Socialism at a time when, according to Charles Raven, the "Church of England had for nearly a century been singularly lacking in spirituality and inspiration." When the Methodists, who had become the church of the industrial masses, broke away from the established church in 1795, "the church expressed her gratitude with a sigh of relief and returned to her slumbers." The Anglo-Catholic Tractarians of the "Oxford Movement" attempted to remold the Church of England into a bulwark against liberalism and reform, and their leader, John Henry Newman, raged against "the shallow and detestable liberalism" that had infringed the vested interests of the church and "gentlemen of county influence." But theologically, the Anglo-Catholics were, as Raven puts it, "looking for a golden age, and with a somewhat pathetic credulity assumed that it was to be traced in the records of undivided Christianity and particularly of the fourth and fifth centuries"; they were laboring "to reconstruct in nineteenth-century England the religion of St. Ambrose or St. Cyril of Alexandria.[2]

For Helen Macfarlane, who had no wish to save the lost soul of Anglicanism, the ideas of founding fathers still did have some relevance—to those who believed in a future "golden age":

> *St. Ambrose* says, in express terms, that "property is a usurpation." *St. Gregory* the Great regards landed proprietors as so

many assassins: "Let them know that the earth, from which they were created, is the common property of all men; and that, therefore, the fruits of the Earth belong indiscriminately to all. Those who make private property of the gift of God, pretend in vain to be innocent. For in retaining the subsistence of the poor, there are the murderers of those who die every day for want of it." What an incendiary vagabond is this "Venerable Father"! *St. John* . . . says "Behold the idea we ought to have concerning rich and avaricious men. They are robbers who beset highways, strip travellers, and then hoard up the property of others in the houses which are their dens." *St. Augustine* says on the subject of inheritance, "Beware of making parental affection a pretext for the augmentation of your possessions. . . . in this way no one would observe the law of God." *St. Basil the Great*, in his Treatise, *De Avarit.* 21, p 328, Paris ed, 1638 asks, "Who is a robber? It is he who appropriates to himself the things which belong to All." *Louis Blanc* is a very tame and moderate person compared with the Communists I have just quoted.[3] [emphasis original]

Frederick Maurice, a leading light of Anglo-Catholicism at Kings College, Oxford, and founder of Christian Socialism, would have had none of this. Although he promoted cooperative workshops, he pronounced nonetheless that "Property is holy; distinction of ranks is holy."[4] Maurice saw his mission not to "appeal to the spirit of a bygone age," but to imbue socialism with "the ever-living and acting Spirit of God." In 1846, Maurice teamed up with John Malcolm Ludlow, a Protestant educated in France who had participated in the enterprises and reform schemes of the French socialists.[5] Whereas Ludlow believed that democracy was necessary to prevent revolution, Maurice was convinced that democracy was impossible without slavery. After all, he asked, wasn't democratic America as much dependent on it as the democracy of Ancient Greece had been? Despite their disagreements, Ludlow accepted Maurice's role as the "Moses" of Christian Socialism; on the day of the Kennington Common demonstration in April 1848, Ludlow, Maurice, and the novelist Charles Kingsley, decided to build a Christian Socialist organization.

In the new period of stability post-1848, the Christian Socialists were able to benefit from the shift in people's interest from political to social activity, such as building friendly societies and cooperative stores. E. Vansittart Neale, a wealthy Christian Socialist and promoter of cooperatives, debated with Ernst Jones in *Notes to the People*. Whereas for Jones the politics of the cooperators often served as a distraction from the needed commitment to the struggle for a democratic republic, for Neale, "monarchical institutions and restricted suffrage, leave to us that personal liberty of action which republican France at present denies to her citizens." Cooperators in France, he claimed, had suffered from "the arbitrary interference of a government chosen by universal suffrage."[6] In 1850, Thornton Leigh Hunt, a Chartist journalist who had joined Neale's Society for Promoting Working Men's Associations, founded with George Henry Lewes a pro-Christian Socialist weekly paper, *The Leader*. When a *Leader* editorial described the *Red Republican* writers as "violent, audacious, and wrathfully earnest," this drew the rejoinder from Macfarlane:

> Ah my dear *Leader*, do you perceive that it is quite impossible for a Red Republican—that is a *sworn foe of existing social arrangements* to be anything other than "violent, audacious, and wrathfully earnest"? . . . I should think we are. Just about as much in earnest as our precursor, "the Sansculotte Jesus" was when He scourged the usurers and money-lenders, and thimble-rigging stockbrokers of Jerusalem."[7] [emphasis original]

Although she often refers to the founder of the Christian religion in comradely terms—as the "gentle Nazarean," the "despised Jewish proletarian," and the "Nazarean carpenter's son"—Macfarlane never uses the name "Jesus Christ," presumably because such "royalist" terminology would have been alien to her conception of the early Christians as the forerunners of *republican* socialist-democracy. The Roman usurpers and the whole tradition based on the Athanasian Creed of the Trinity and the Incarnation were for her, "pagan rather than Christian"—pagan, in this sense, meaning an amalgam of the practices of the Egyptian, Hebrew, and Roman priesthoods. Macfarlane records a report by "one reverend gent" that in his district of London he found "the moral condition deplorable. Socialism, Infidelity, Rationalism, and indifference prevail to a fearful extent. One individual, when warned to flee the wrath to come said 'let us hope there is no such place as hell-fire. . . . we have too much misery to endure here, for God to think of punishing us hereafter.'" Another "state priest" is reported as accounting for the spread of Mormonism in his district "by the preference men have for the marvelous and the desire of possessing heaven on earth, toiling in our rumbling manufactories." Macfarlane comments:

> The Mormons are subject to a very strict, semi-military discipline, but every member of a Mormon Association is certain of being fed, housed, and clothed. . . . I believe Joe Smith's tenets partake somewhat of the marvelous, but this Mormon apostate must have been a stunning fellow, if he produced anything more astonishing than the Creed of St. Athanasius.[8]

The 1840s had seen a building boom in churches not seen since the Norman Conquest. The influx of Irish laborers had invigorated Roman Catholicism in England and in response, the Anglican-Catholic Tractarians had been building churches in the lavish styles of Catholicism and reintroducing the Mass in the hope of converting the children of the London Irish. In "Signs of the Times: Redstockings versus Lawn-Sleeves," Macfarlane comments on the growing concern of the Anglican state church over "Popish attempts to poach on her sacred manor." Dismissing Anglican claims to defend the freedom of the "intellect and soul," she hails the row between the two churches as "among the most important and cheering signs of the times. Because it shows that the world of Ideas is taking the same direction as the world of Facts. The inward world is obeying the same law as the outward world."[9]

At the time Helen Macfarlane was writing for the *Red Republican*, the editor of the *Leader*, George Henry Lewes, had a blossoming literary and marital partnership with George Eliot (then still known as Marian Evans) at the *Westminster Review*. Evans also contributed to the *Leader* under a pseudonym.

While there is no evidence that Macfarlane and Evans ever met, what they had in common is noteworthy. In 1842 Evans had decided that the "system of doctrines" upheld by the Church of England was based on "histories consisting of mingled fiction and truth" and was "dishonourable to God and most pernicious in its influence on individual and social happiness."[10] Macfarlane had come to similar conclusions. Both were studying and translating German philosophy: Evans had translated *The Life of Jesus* by David Strauss and would later translate Strauss's fellow "Young Hegelian," Lugwig Feuerbach; Macfarlane had translated Marx and Engels (also "Young Hegelians") for the *Red Republican*, as well as a little bit of Hegel for the *Democratic Review*. Both women were living in London during that year and writing for periodicals whose offices were on the same street and whose circles of associates were by no means mutually exclusive. Eliot's recent biographer, Karl Frederick, suggests that it is possible that Marian Evans met Marx in 1850: an associate of the *Westminster Review*, Andrew Johnson, took Marx with him on a visit to the journal's office on the Strand to offer the journal some translations of poetry by Marx's friend Ferdinand Freiligrath. (According to Frederick, "Marian was not happy about this," because while she had some sympathy for "moderate" European radicals, such as Mazzini and Louis Blanc, she thought of Freiligrath as "extreme.")[11]

Not only would Evans and Macfarlane have disagreed politically, but probably philosophically as well; Evans's interest in post-Hegelian German philosophy was, by 1850, giving way to Auguste Comte 's proposition that theology and metaphysics were being superceded by a new "religion" based on "observable," "scientific" facts. This "positivism" excluded any questioning of underlying social forces or speculation on ultimate social goals, and opted for "wise resignation" to existing social evils until such as time as social equilibrium—rather than social conflict—could produce "positive remedies." In contrast to Evans, the political perspectives resulting from

Macfarlane's encounter with German philosophy, to which we turn next, ruled out the possibility of social equilibrium:

> This world of thought is rapidly breaking up into two camps: the one containing the partizans [sic] of despotic authority; the other, the champions of unlimited free thought; of unlimited, unchecked, intellectual and moral development.[12]

Notes

1. *The Collected Works of Samuel Taylor Coleridge, Volume 6: Lay Sermons* (Princeton: Princeton University Press, 1972).

2. Charles Raven, *Christian Socialism 1848–54,* (London: Frank Cass, 1920), 19.

3. *Democratic Review,* June 1850.

4. Edward Norman, *The Victorian Christian Socialists* (Cambridge: Cambridge University Press, 1987), 14–34. Raven, *Christian Socialism,* 20.

5. Raven, *Christian Socialism,* 91.

6. *Notes,* 470–76.

7. *Red Republican,* July 20, 1850.

8. *Red Republican,* November 9, 1850.

9. *Friend of the People,* December 21 and 28, 1850.

10. Karl Frederick, *George Eliot: A Biography* (London: Harper-Collins, 1995), 54.

11. Frederick, *George Eliot,* 133.

12. *Friend of the People,* December 28, 1850.

8

Helen Macfarlane's Interpretation of Hegel

> Axioms in philosophy are not axioms until they are proved upon our pulses."
>
> —John Keats

German Idealism and the Crisis in Christianity

Against David Hume and the skeptics, Immanuel Kant (1724–1804) argued that the world of phenomena could be perceived, understood, and reasoned about through the mediation of transcendental, a priori, categories of thought. Summarizing Kant's "Revolution," Heinrich Heine writes:

> Once upon a time Reason, like a sun, circled around the world of appearances, and sought to illuminate it; but Kant bade Reason to stand still, and now the world of appearance revolves around and is illumined by it.[1]

Kant sees morality as the realm of freedom, as opposed to a world of nature governed by necessity. In Kant's moral philosophy, his "categorical imperatives" are formulated according to the maxim that any action by an individual ought to be universally valid. Kant, in arriving at his a priori truths of Pure Reason independently of "facts," also denies that there are any a priori—or factual—grounds for religious belief. He does, however, come up with the idea of a "moral governor of the world" as a postulate of practical reason, without which the will of the acting subject would have no definite object and would be left only with the empty forms of the law: "It concerns us not so much to know what God is in Himself (his nature), as what he is for us as moral beings."[2]

In the real world of struggles over justice and equality, the various moral imperatives might appear to be locked in conflict with each other. But such problems only persisted in the absence of proper education on the Moral Law, or because of outdated social structures and dogmatic religious authority, or simply because of the "crooked wood" that would always constitute the "unknowable," *noumenal* self of the human.

Hegel objects to the great divide that Kant puts between phenomena and *noumena*, between reason and the "thing-in-itself." Hegel agrees with Kant on the inseparability of morality and freedom, but he sees Kant's idealism as overly subjective. For Hegel, "only that which is an *object* of Freedom can be called an Idea" (emphasis mine). As a modern "realist," Hegel, like Kant, dismisses all ontological or cosmological proofs of the existence of a personal God and also rejects the "rationalist" method, which abandons philosophy and wages war on religious dogma by appeal to the "mechanical sciences" of chemistry, biology, meteorology, etc. Hegel argues: "The true cognition of God begins with our knowing that things in their *immediate* being have no truth"[3] (emphasis mine).

Hegel points out that Christianity only survived because of the investigations by its earliest philosophers in Alexandria into the works of the Greek philosophers, written several centuries earlier: Plato and Aristotle had combined a "conception of the infinite" with a "concrete idea of the spirit" and had thereby comprehended "the purport of the Christian religion."[4] What Christianity had contributed was a new conception of freedom; it is this issue that Helen Macfarlane takes up in her discussion of Hegel's introduction to *Lectures on the History of Philosophy*, a work few Marxists have ever paid much attention to. One who did, Lenin, in his *Hegel Notebooks* of 1914 and 1915, praises the "strict historicity" of Hegel's approach, which attempts to show that "the sequence of the systems of philosophy in history is the same as the sequence of the Notion-determinations of the idea [as presented in Hegel's *Science of Logic*]." Lenin, however, gets very impatient with Hegel's observations on the historical/philosophical development of religion in his introduction to the *Lectures*. He complains that they are "Extremely lengthy, empty, and tedious on the relation of philosophy to religion in general, an introduction of almost two-hundred pages—impossible."[5] Lenin, unlike Macfarlane sixty-five years earlier, belonged to a left that sought to divide philosophy into idealism and materialism and to claim the latter for the cause of "progress." Following the green light given by Engels's *Ludwig Feuerbach and the End of Classical German Philosophy*, post-Marx Marxists adopted, in effect, a philosophical positivism drawn from the findings of nineteenth-century science. Discussion of religion was confined to sociological "explanations" of how religious belief "reflected" material forces. But for Macfarlane in 1850, despite her dismissal of all creeds, sects, and churches, the revolutionary undercurrents of Christianity were objective and historical:

> In the antique world, the position of man was determined by the accident of birth. As a citizen of Athens, or of Rome, he was free. But these Athenian and Roman citizens denied the same rights to men belonging to all other nations, whom they contemptuously styled barbarians. They enslaved these other men, or used them up as chattels—in a variety of ways, according as it was found profitable or convenient; precisely as the "free and enlightened citizens of America" do the coloured men at the present day. . . . Neither in the religion, nor in the philosophy of the ancient world, do we find the divinity of human nature expressed. Among the rich variety of forms assumed by the antique civilisation, there is not one which expresses this fundamental idea of Christianity or democracy, either in a mythical or speculative form. The ancient philosophers left many questions untouched which now occupy a great space in the territory of speculation. For example [Macfarlane then quotes Hegel (her translation)]:
>
>> The enquiries into the faculty of cognition, into the opposition of subjectivity and objectivity, were unknown in Plato's time.

> The absolute independence of the personality, its existence for
> and through itself, were quite unknown to Plato. Man had not
> then returned—so to speak—into himself, had not thoroughly
> investigated his own nature. This individual subject was indeed
> independent, free—but was conscious of this only as an isolated
> fact. The Athenian, the Roman, knew he was free. But that man,
> as such, is free—as a human being, is born free—was unknown
> to Plato and to Aristotle, to Cicero, and to the Roman jurists, al-
> though this conception alone is the source of all jurisprudence.
> In Christianity we find, for the first time, the individual per-
> sonal soul depicted as possessing an infinite, absolute value.
> God wills the salvation of all men.[6]

The unity of natural and spiritual existence—which Hegel
designates as "the innate freedom of Man"—had thus only been
implicit in the philosophies of Antiquity. In truth, Hegel contends,
this unity "must also exist for the sensuous, representative consciousness. . . . it must appear," and does so in the Christian religion. Although Hegel doesn't reject the Holy Trinity as such, he
restates and resituates the Christian concept of the Incarnation
within the wholeness of the movement of the Idea. Hegel points
out that whereas in the Islamic and Judaic religions the authority
of the all-powerful One appears as an abstract and external force,
in the Christian Incarnation the relationship of God with Nature
is revealed through the sensuous and concrete images of pictorial
thought ("*Vorstellung*"). Spirit is posited as pure Identity that
"separates itself from itself" in order to enter "existence for and
in itself as contrasted with the Universal." In Christianity, "that
antithetical form of Spirit is the Son of God; reduced to limited
and particular conception. It is the World-Nature and Finite
Spirit: Finite Spirit itself therefore is posited as a constituent element [moment] of the Divine Being. Man is therefore comprehended in the Idea of God."[7]

The passage from Hegel quoted earlier by Macfarlane continues:

> In this religion [Christianity] we find the doctrine that the
> whole human race is equal in the sight of God, redeemed from
> bondage, and introduced into a state of Christian freedom by
> Jesus. These modes of representation make freedom indepen-
> dent of rank, birth, cultivation, and the like; and the progress

which has been made by this means is immense. Yet this mode of viewing the matter is somewhat different from the fact that freedom is an indispensable element in the conception—man. The undefined feeling of this fact has worked for centuries in the dark; the instinct for freedom had produced the most terrible revolutions, but the idea of the innate freedom of man— this knowledge of his own nature—is not old."[8]

This new knowledge, in Macfarlane's commentary, is the philosophic expression of the Democratic Idea that had always been implicit in Christianity:

These two modes of viewing the matter are the necessary compliments of each other. The one mode is imaginative, the other intellectual; the one is religious, the other philosophical. The first mode presents the democratic idea in the form of a myth; the second presents it in the more appropriate and developed form of a conception—as a product of pure reason. But they both belong to the modern world. In the whole civilization of the human race, there is not a trace of the democratic idea to be found, until the appearance of the Nazarean. This being the case, might we not reasonably expect that the forms assumed by modern civilisation would be essentially different from those assumed by the antique culture? Vain expectation! "The centuries are conspirators against the sanity and majesty of the soul," says an American writer. We are haunted by the ghosts of the old dead nations and cultures.

(The "American writer" is Ralph Waldo Emerson: "Is the acorn better than the oak, which is its fullness and completion? Is the parent better than the child into whom he has cast his ripened being? Whence, then, this worship of the past? The centuries are conspirators against the sanity and authority of the soul.")[9]

At the "popular" level, according to Hegel in the *Science of Logic*, the "fact" of freedom as "an indispensable element" is expressed as feeling. But "feeling" and all human behavior has its own logic:

Logic itself is just man's peculiar nature. But if nature in general is opposed, as physical, to what is mental, then it must be said that Logic is rather that something Super-natural which enters into all the natural *behaviour* of man—Feeling, Intuition, Desire, Need, Impulse—and thereby alone transforms it all to something human—to ideas and purposes.[10] [emphasis mine]

Pantheism

I believe in Spinoza's God who reveals Himself in the orderly harmony of what exists, not in a God who concerns himself with fates and actions of human beings.

—Albert Einstein[11]

Both Hegel and Kant were accused in their own lifetimes of undermining religion, because in both of their philosophies Christian theology is seemingly impaled on the altar of reason and science. In the case of Hegel, some opponents saw an underlying pantheism in his philosophy and charged him with "Spinozism."

In contrast with Descartes' dualistic separation of thought and being, the monist philosophy of Baruch Spinoza (1632–1677) denies that there is any world of ideas, forms, or eternal moral truths existing separately from a world of natural objects; in Spinoza's writings, the terms "God" and "Nature" are interchangeable. For Spinoza, thought and extensions of thought (being) are understood as essential attributes of an infinite absolute substance, which exists in itself and is conceived by itself. The physical shapes of all natural objects in the universe are modifications—or "modes"—of the universal attribute of three-dimensionality. Thus humans are modes of divine attributes in a physical sense, but also in the "spiritual" sense as well: the derived modes of the attribute of thought are manifested in the "pure" universal truths of science, mathematics, and philosophy. All individual things are only conceived "in and through something else" and have only a distant causal relation with the Absolute. Although every determination of a mode represents a negation and a limit (to determine one's property, for example, is to define its limit and deny it to somebody else), every mode can be referred back to the One

Substance that is the "inner cause" of everything. The sole freedom for individuals lies in recognizing themselves in this subordinate relation to "divine attributes"; only in this way can they escape from the "slavery" of passions, sensuous images, and limited thought.

Spinoza refutes the charge made by his religious opponents that in his philosophy God, as the originator of all existence, must also be seen as "responsible" for existing evil. On the contrary, he argues, only that which has an "essential content" can be causally attributed to the divine One. Taking the example of Nero's murder of his mother, Spinoza poses the question: "Wherein then consists Nero's crime? In nothing else but that he proved himself ungrateful, merciless, and disobedient. But it is certain that all this expresses no essence, and therefore God was not the cause of it." God, as the self-causing cause of everything, was the cause of Nero's action and intention, but it was only Nero's lack of loyalty and mercy as *an individual* that constituted the crime.

Hegel recognizes Spinoza's idea of "substance" as the "abstract unity which mind is in itself" and as the essential beginning of *all* philosophy; a restatement of the pre-Socratic idea of "being" first formulated by Anaxagoras and Parmenides:

> When man begins to philosophize, the soul must commence by bathing in this ether of the One Substance, in which all that man has held as true has disappeared; this negation of all that is particular . . . is the liberation of the mind and its absolute foundation."[12]

Hegel adds, however, that Spinoza's "return" to essential beginnings goes beyond "the simple universal of Plato"; though it has "come to know the absolute opposition of Notion and Being," it abolishes the modern Cartesian separation of corporeality and the thinking "I." Hegel sees Spinoza's conceptions as "in the main true and well-grounded," but lacking in "their true concrete sense." Hegel, in situating the conceptions of Substance, Attribute, and Mode within the syllogistic form of the Universal, Particular, and Individual, criticizes Spinoza's conception of the finite individual "mode" as a "retreat" from the universal. The individual merely "enters into external existence with what is 'other,'" and is trapped in a "false individuality" that lacks the subjectivity of Being-for-self, and thus vanishes into existence without a "return" to the universal. The individual, lacking the "principle of personality," is left homeless and does not "rise" through the particular to the unity of the Notion. Hegel sees Spinoza's concept of negation as one-sided; substance, for Hegel, is also *subject*. Whereas Spinoza's negation is infinite, Hegel's "absolute negativity" represents at the same time the "negation of the negation," working through history and philosophy.

Helen Macfarlane's self-proclaimed pantheism, which makes no mention of Spinoza, is a Hegelian, universalist negation of all religious dogmas, whether ancient or modern. In Macfarlane's view, the Reformation had long run its course and Protestantism had itself become such an impediment to forward movement that it too was now in a state of political, philosophical, and spiritual crisis:

> Now, one effect of this spiritual development will be that the partizans of despotism (who are also invariably the upholders of secular despotism) will no longer be able to masquerade among the defenders of liberty. Protestantism must now accept the reformation of the nineteenth century, or enter the camp of the Past. . . .
>
> Here then we see the dawn of the new reformation . . . in the form of two frightful bugbears; on the one hand, appearing as catholicism; on the other, as "Rationalism with infidelity and pantheism in its train." But the days of orthodox protestantism are numbered. The human mind has not been standing still for the last three hundred years. Men are beginning to perceive that this system satisfies neither the heart nor the head; neither the imagination or the intellect. For it swept away all the poetry of the Christian Mythos and gave a death blow to the art of the middle ages. It left us with nothing but a set of abstract creeds and dogmas professedly based upon another set of questionable sagas and hearsays . . . scholastic formulas, which . . . have been outgrown . . . and are now so many impediments [to] spiritual development.

Yet as every historical appearance, every manifestation of thought, is (in its place) both useful and inevitable—or so in other words, as every fact has its meaning, you will necessarily ask, what is the meaning of Protestantism? It is a state of transition. It is the stepping stone for the human mind in its progress from deism to *pantheism*—that is, from a belief in some things, in the divinity of one being or of one man, to a belief in the divinity of All beings, of All men—in the holiness of All things. . . . The inward or spiritual compromise between these principles of the past and the future, resulted in the outward and temporal compromise between the same. . . . All history bears witness to the truth of an old saying, "as a man is, so are his gods" or conversely that the actions of man—his laws, forms of government, art, literature . . . in a word, the phases of civilization, prevalent amongst any people, are directly derived from its theology. If we know the fundamental principle of any given theology, we can at once predict the amount of secular freedom, or the degree of political and social development, which is compatible with a belief in that theology. Thus we find feudal despotism the prevailing form of government in Catholic countries."[13]

Macfarlane here echoes Hegel's criticism of Catholicism, a religion he judged to be fundamentally "opposed to a rational constitution" in which "Government and People" could "reciprocate." Hegel, nevertheless, found it necessary to recognize the historical objectivity of the Catholic Church when he came up against F. Jacobi (1743–1819). Jacobi, taking on the arguments of the materialist enlightenment, argued that Reason could do no more than illuminate the conditions of what is conditioned, that science could provide only finite, quantitative knowledge of determinations. If everything that is conditioned must be presupposed by the unconditioned—which neither Reason nor science can define or determine—then Nature, as human nature, must, according to Jacobi, presuppose God. This being the case, any relationship with the unconditioned comes about only through inward revelation, not Reason. Whereas for Kant, faith was a postulate of practical reason for the solution of the contradiction between the World and the Ideal of the Good, for Jacobi faith was immediate knowledge.[14]

Hegel sees Jacobi as leading an irrationalist revolt against both tradition and reason: "the Christian faith comprises in it an authority of the Church; but the faith of Jacobi's philosophy has no other authority than that of personal revelation."[15]

Hegel points out that

> the Christian faith is a copious body of objective truth, a system of knowledge and doctrine; while the scope of the philosophic faith [Jacobi] is so utterly indefinite, that, while it has room for the faith of the Christian, it equally admits belief in the divinity of the Dalai Lama, the ox, or the monkey.[16]

Hegel sees Jacobi's assault on universality and objectivity as a reaction to the spiritual crisis and disorganization within Protestantism, whose origins lay in the "tormenting uncertainty" that Calvinism had introduced into the minds of individuals. Similarly, for Macfarlane, in "the regions of spiritual compromise, of doubt and fluctuation, of unrest, of weariness and vexation of soul—the region of protestantism . . . [there] is no fundamental principle, upon which a reasonable creature could find a firm footing." She continues:

> All sects hedge me in with limitations. I cannot move a step in any direction without running into some creed, or catechism, or formula, which rises up like a wall between the unhappy sectarians and the rest of the universe; beyond which it is forbidden to look on pain of damnation, or worse.[17]

The official churches and the sects were all part of the same problem, because "an infallible book is assumed as the basis of religious faith, yet without having any professedly infallible interpreter" and "covertly, every sect assumes its articles, confession or creed, to be the infallible interpretor." Anyone who refuses any particular sect's interpretation is "immediately denounced as an 'infidel scoffer.'" It was "no wonder" that the Catholics held sway: by standing above the myriad "interpretations" of the Book, which all just confuse the masses, and by pointing to the Holy Church of Rome as the "perpetually inspired witness" capable of organizing a "universal religion" for all.

Although "opposed to a rational constitution," Catholicism was itself by no means free from the ferment of ideas and the passion for freedom; it must have been very striking to Macfarlane that here, too, dissent took the form of pantheism. F. R. H. Lamennais (1782–1854), originally known as a somewhat reactionary Catholic romantic and mystic, greeted the mobilization of the Parisian proletariat behind the barricades of 1830 with the words, "Can you not hear the breath of God?" His book *Words of a Believer* published in France in 1834 expressed a form of populist Christian socialism. His works were praised in Harney's *Democratic Review* and extracts from his writings appeared in the *Red Republican*. Hegel, in his introduction to the *Philosophy of History*, notes:

> Eloquently and impressively has the Abbe Lamennais reckoned it among the criteria of the true religion, that it must be the universal—that is Catholic—and the oldest in date; and the Congregation has labored zealously and diligently in France towards rendering such assertions no longer mere pulpit tirades and authoritative dicta, such as were deemed sufficient formerly. The religion of Buddha—a god-man—which has prevailed to such an enormous extent, has especially attracted attention.[18]

Close reading of Macfarlane's expositions of "pantheism" shows no direct traces of Lamennais; it does, however, show the influence of Heinrich Heine (1797–1856). A pupil of Hegel in Berlin and later a friend and collaborator of Karl Marx, Heine issued a provocative defense of the "New Pantheism" in 1835:

> In man divinity attains self consciousness—and the latter in turn is revealed through man. This is achieved not in or through a single individual, but in and through the totality of mankind—so that every man comprehends and represents in himself only a portion of the God-Universe, but all men together comprehend and represent it in its totality—in ideas well as reality.

On the political orientation of pantheism, Heine continues:

The political revolution which is based on the principles of French materialism will find no enemies in the pantheists, but rather allies who derive their convictions from a deeper source, from a religious synthesis. . . . [The] divinity of man manifests itself also in his body. Human misery destroys or abases the body, which is the image of God. . . . We interpret the great words of the Revolution which St. Just pronounced, *"le pain est le droit du peuple,"* as meaning *"le pain est le droit divin de l'homme."* We do not contend for the human rights of the people, but for the divine rights of man. In this, and in many other respects, we differ from the men of the Revolution. We do not wish to be sans-culottes, or frugal citizens, or economical presidents. We establish a democracy of equally glorious, equally holy and equally happy gods. You ask for simple dress, austere manners and unseasoned joys. We, on the other hand, demand nectar and ambrosia, purple raiments, costly perfumes, luxury and splendor, dances of laughing nymphs, music and comedy. Oh, do not be angry, virtuous republicans! To your censorious reproaches, we say with the fool in Shakespeare, "Dost thou think because thou art virtuous, there shall be no more cakes and ale?

And he concludes:

We have, in fact outgrown deism. We are free and do not need a tyrant with thunder. We have come of age and do not need paternal supervision. We are not the bungled handiwork of a great mechanic. Deism is a religion for slaves, children, Genevans, and watchmakers.[19]

Macfarlane echoes Heine's words in her call for a "Republic without helots, without poor, without classes. . . . A society, such indeed as the world has never seen—not only of free men, but of free women; a society of equally, holy, equally blessed gods." (The phrase "Republic without helots" comes from August Blanqui's celebrated speech to the French court in 1849.) Pantheism, in Macfarlane's definition, is:

The sublime and cheering doctrine of man's infinity—as the oak lies folded up in the acorn. . . . The divine nature (or at least in a manifestation of it which is found only in man) is common to us all. . . . We are bound to do to others, as we would they should do to us. This rule is universally valid, without distinction of birth, age, rank, sex, country, colour, cultivation, or the like.

This resembles Hegel's view of Christianity: as "the doctrine that the whole human race is equal in the sight of God, redeemed from bondage, and introduced into a state of Christian freedom . . . independent of rank, birth, cultivation and the like." Macfarlane writes: "Upon the doctrine of man's divinity, rests the distinction between a person and a thing . . . the most heinous crime I can perpetrate is invading the personality of my brother man. . . . Red Republicanism . . . is a protest against the using up of man by man."

For Macfarlane, pantheism is the same "democratic idea" that had undergone many historical incarnations through the ages:

The idea of perfect Liberty, of Equality, and Fraternity—the divine idea of love, incarnate in the gentle Nazarean, is the idea we earnestly worship. It freed itself from the dead weight of a lifeless Past in the days of Luther, bursting forth from under the accumulated rubbish of ages, like waters of life—like a fountain to refresh the wanderer fainting in desert places: it found an expression free from all symbols, sagas, and historical forms, in the "Declaration of the Rights of Man," by Maximilian Robespierre, and in the immortal pages of the "Contrat Social" and "Emile." The next step in the development of this divine idea will be its practical realization: the Ethico-political regeneration of society.[20]

Since Robespierre's time, Macfarlane writes in her first article for the *Democratic Review*, the Idea had also passed through the German philosophy:

This great work had been begun by the Lollards and other heretics of the middle ages, but its accomplishment was reserved for Luther . . . that unique and profound investigation into the nature of man, which, conducted by a phalanx of modern philosophers, was terminated by Hegel, the last and greatest. The result of this investigation was the democratic idea, but as thought, not in the inadequate form of a history or saga. As Hegel expresses it, "Freedom is a necessary element in the conception, man." . . . The next step in the history of this idea, will be its practical realization.[21]

The earlier-quoted passage from Hegel's introduction to *The Lectures on the History of Philosophy* and Macfarlane's commentary on it raises an interesting question for Hegel scholars: was Helen Macfarlane the *first* translator and commentator on Hegel in the English-speaking world? According to J. H. Muirhead, in the 1928 essay "How Hegel Came to England":

> It was not until 1855, when an English translation of part of the Logic [*The Subjective Logic of Hegel*, translated by H. Sloman and J. Wallon], that any word of his was available to students ignorant of German.[22]

Another Hegel scholar, Peter Nicholson, points out that the Sloman–Wallon work was, in fact, a mere "translation of a French paraphrase and compilation of Hegel's ideas, not a real translation of Hegel at all." The first real and complete published translation of any of Hegel's works into English was, therefore, *The Philosophy of History*, translated in 1857 by John Sibree, an associate of George Eliot.[23]

According to Muirhead, "Up to the middle of the [eighteen] fifties it may be said that no intelligible word had been spoken by British writers as to the place and significance of Hegel's work." Muirhead, like all commentators on the nineteenth-century "British Hegelians," misses Macfarlane's first translation of Hegel. And, as we have seen, Helen Macfarlane's writings of 1850 speak much more than one "intelligible word" on the subject and constitute a lost prehistory of "British-Hegelian" thought.

Notes

1. Heinrich Heine, *Self Portrait and Other Prose Writings* (Secaucus, N.J.: 1948), 465.

2. Immanuel Kant, *Religion within the Limits of Reason Alone* (New York: Harper and Row, 1960), 130.

3. G. W. F. Hegel, *Hegel's Logic* (Oxford: Clarendon Press, 1975), 177.

4. G. W. F. Hegel, *Philosophy of History* (New York: Dover, 1956), 330.

5. V. I. Lenin, *Collected Works Vol. 38*, (Moscow: Progress Publishers, 1972), 247–48.

6. *Democratic Review*, May 1850.

7. Hegel, *Philosophy of History*, 330.

8. Sourced as *"Hegel, vol 13, p93. Sammt Werke*. Berlin. Edit. by Professors Marheineke, Michelet, Hotho, and others."

9. Ralph Waldo Emerson, "Self-Reliance," in *Essays* (Boston, 1841. Republished in 1847 as *Essays: First Series*). Available online at www.emersoncentral.com/selfreliance.htm.

10. G. W. F. Hegel, *Science of Logic* (Atlantic Highlands, N.J.: Humanities Press, 1989), 31–32.

11. P. A. Schipp, ed., *Albert Einstein: Philosopher-Scientist* (LaSalle, Ill.: Open Court), 659–660.

12. G. W. F. Hegel, *Lectures on the History of Philosophy III* (Lincoln: University of Nebaska Press, 1995), 257–58.

13. *Friend of the People*, December 21, 1850.

14. Hegel, *Lectures III*, 410–23.

15. Hegel, *Hegel's Logic*, para 63.

16. Hegel, *Hegel's Logic*, para 63.

17. *Democratic Review*, June 12, 1850.

18. Hegel, *Philosophy of History*, 58.

19. Heine, *Self Portrait*, 560.

20. *Red Republican*, July 20, 1850.

21. *Democratic Review*, June 1850.

22. H. Muirhead, *The Platonic Tradition in Anglo-Saxon Philosophy* (London: Allen & Unwin, 1931).

23. Peter P. Nicholson, Review of P. Robbins, "The British Hegelians 1875–1925," *Bulletin of the Hegel Society of Great Britain*, no. 3, 1983.

9

Antigone in 1848

Hegel argued that philosophy must sometimes exercise "audacity." So also for Helen Macfarlane must its practical realization:

> We, who rally round the Red Flag, are reproached with entertaining the nefarious design of completely destroying the existing order of things, with the desire of totally abolishing the present system of society,—for the purpose, it is said of putting some fantastic dream, some wild utopia of our own in place of long established and venerable institutions.

The "accusers" were "bankers, cottonspinners, landowners," as well as "'superior women,' educated according to the recipes of Mrs. Ellis for making 'admirable wives and mothers'":

> We are low people certainly; disreputable vagabonds without doubt. In ancient times we were accounted "the enemies of the human race," accused of setting fire to Rome. . . . I am happy to say we still retain our old reputation . . . and have not failed to follow the laudable example of our precursors in Roman times. . . . Yet even in England, this shopkeeping country of middle-class respectability there are a few of us belonging to the "better sort" who have repudiated all claim to be considered respectable, because for them the words Justice and Love are not mere empty sounds without a meaning; because they

say—like Antigone in Sophocles—the laws of God are not of today, nor of yesterday, they exist from all eternity.[1]

In this remarkable unfurling of the Red Flag as the enactment of "laws of God" that "exist from all eternity," Macfarlane seems to have taken onboard Hegel's analysis of Sophocles' tragedy *Antigone*. The dramatic action of this play takes place in the aftermath of the battle for control of the city of Thebes, in which Antigone's two brothers, Polyneices and Eteocles, have killed each other in rivalry. Eteocles' victorious ally, his uncle King Creon, inherits the throne and decrees that, while Eteocles should be buried with full honors, the "rebel" Polyneices should be left outside the walls of the city to be eaten by the birds. Antigone refuses to accept this dishonoring of her brother. Despite threats from Creon that he will bury her alive, she buries Polyneices according to the tribal religion and she wins Creon's son Haemon over to her side. The conflict ends in disaster for all concerned.

Hegel describes how the dramatic clash in *Antigone* "takes place between two irreconcilable principles": on the one hand, the Moral Law of the State, which is cruel, but nonetheless, historically progressive; on the other hand, the law of natural family honor, based on the kinship principles of a stateless society. As quoted by Hegel and echoed by Macfarlane, Antigone says of this natural law:

Not now, indeed, nor yesterday, but for aye
It lives, and no man knows what time it came.[2]

George Lukacs, in *The Young Hegel*, shows how Hegel saw *Antigone* as a precursor of the "tragedy in the realm of the ethical" he saw unfolding in capitalism. Hegel feared that because great wealth seemed to be "indissolubly connected with the direst poverty," the powers of the "lower world" (as expressed in the "laws" of political economy) were becoming inverted with the "higher world" (the Ethical State) and threatening to dissolve the "bonds uniting the whole people."[3] The dialectical tension of the play develops because the supposedly less "civilized" of the two colliding forces gains, in Hegel's words, a "self-conscious actual universality." Antigone does not just stand up to the new state. She also stands out as an individual from those in her community "who think as I do but dare not speak." Antigone holds her defiance as more important than her life and in breaking the silence she breaks the bonds holding the state together.

Lukacs argues that Hegel, in a sense, anticipated the anthropologist Bachofen, who first saw in *Antigone* and the *Oresteia* the conflict between the bonds of the matriarchy of the old tribal society ("blood-bond") and the patriarchal Greek statism ("bed-bond"). In the old Chthonian religions the earth itself, which brings forth life, is female; but in the patriarchal Apollonian culture the senior goddess, Athene, is born from the head of Zeus. This shift in mythology reflects the replacement of the clans' common ownership principle by private property and as the increasing power of males in controlling "movable property" in the form of slaves.[4]

Raya Dunayevskaya, addressing socialist feminists fighting for "autonomy" from the Old Left in the 1970s, argues that Hegel's analysis of *Antigone* expresses how the individual's experience in revolt can lead to a new subjectivity "purified" of all that "interferes with its universality," in which the prevailing "principle" is an objective "autonomy" of self-liberation. Dunayevskaya, who like Macfarlane identifies the Idea of Freedom with the Idea of History, freed from its narrow bourgeois horizon, praises Lukacs's restatement of the importance of the Hegelian dialectic for understanding Marx's humanism, but rejects Lukacs's "fetishism" of the "vanguard party" as mediator of class consciousness. Dunayevskaya points out that post-Marx Marxists tend to limit "subjectivity" to mere comprehension of an abstract universal of "socialism" as negation of capitalism—which in reality had ended up as Stalinism and other forms of statism. But the second subjectivity—as "negation of the negation"—contains, she suggests, the objectivity of real struggles by real human beings.[5]

These twentieth-century interpretations of Hegel's analysis of *Antigone* illustrate its ongoing significance in revolutionary thinking. In Helen Macfarlane's case, in 1850, it resurfaces in an article on the visit to London in July 1850 by Baron Von Haynau, the Austrian Field Marshall and war criminal. In 1848, the Imperial Army had been driven out of Hungary and independence from Vienna declared. But under the terms of the Holy Alliance, Czar Nicholas I had sent Russian forces into Hungary to restore Hapsburg rule. Afterward, Haynau had unleashed his own troops on the defeated Hungarian population in an orgy of reprisals. When in July 1850, Haynau, during a semi-official London visit, called at the Barclays and Perkins brewery on Bankside, word got around the Chartist-supporting workers that the "Butcher Haynau " was in their midst. The workers set upon him and attempted to drown him in a barrel of beer; he narrowly escaped with his life and had to be rescued by a squad of constables. When the *Morning Post* asked, "How is it that the labouring class, once profoundly indifferent to what was taking place in foreign countries . . . have suddenly become so sensitive?" it drew the following response from Macfarlane:

> Let us look at the other side. A hoary-headed old ruffian orders women to be stripped naked, and flogged till nearly dead, by a set of savage soldiers. And these executors of his lawless will were not half so brutal as "this noble and knightly gentleman"— this Austrian commander-in-chief, who, in some instances, personally superintended the civilized and refined operation. Of what terrible revolting crime had these unhappy women been guilty? They had aided their husbands, their fathers, their brothers, in the Hungarian and Italian insurrections. . . . Had I been present, when those brave proletarians gave this ruffian his deserts, I should have certainly dissuaded "the mob from using violence," that is, from actually lying hands on him. I would have said brothers, your hands are hardened and blackened from honest toil. Do not pollute them from touching that beast. Take mops and brooms, sweep him out as you do other kinds of dirt. Like to like. Filth to filth. Haynau to the common sewer!

The Hungarian women, Macfarlane points out, "had aided those to whom they were bound by every natural and legal tie," as part of the struggle for Freedom. Like Antigone, it seems, they had upheld a "higher law" than that laid down by the state. And "it lives." In another article she links the "Holy Spirit of truth" with the guidance of the "Nazarean" toward

> a pure Democracy, where freedom and equality will be the acknowledged birth right of every human being; the golden age, sung by the poets and prophets of all times and nations, from Hesiod and Isaiah, to Cervantes and Shelley; the "Paradise," which was never lost, for it lives—not backwards, in the infancy and youth of humanity—but in the future.[6]

Macfarlane's recognition of her own subjectivity as one of the "few of us belonging to the 'better sort,'" who (as she puts it in reference to Antigone) had defected to the side of the oppressed, comes from Marx. *The Communist Manifesto*, as translated by Macfarlane, celebrates the fact that "a part of the bourgeoisie is joining the proletariat, and particularly a part of bourgeois ideologists, or middle-class thinkers who have attained a theoretical knowledge of the whole historical movement."

Notes

1. *Red Republican*, October 12, 1850.

2. *Red Republican*, November 9, 1850. The lines from Sophocles are quoted by Hegel in the *Phenomenology of Mind*, 452.

3. Lukacs, *The Young Hegel*, 411–12.

4. George Thompson, *Aeschylus and Athens* (London: Lawrence and Wishart, 1941), 47–48.

5. Raya Dunayevskaya, "Talk on Hegel and Antigone, January 4th 1977," *Raya Dunayevskaya Collection*, Walter P. Reuther Library at Wayne State University, Detriot, Michigan. University. Dunayevskaya, *The Power of Negativity. Selected Writings on the Dialectic in Hegel and Marx* (Lanham, Md.: Lexington, 2002), 213–23.

6. *Red Republican*, June 22, 1850.

10

Thomas Carlyle and the Red Republicans

Waging War on the Poor

Scottish-born Thomas Carlyle (1795–1881) was a popular and long-lasting literary opponent of liberalism, democracy, and modernity. Around 1830, Carlyle fell briefly under the spell of the "utopian" French Saint-Simonians. But while the utopian socialists projected a future work ethic fuelled by wondrous scientific innovations, Carlyle drew on the values of "tradition." His 1843 book, *Past and Present*, portrays the medieval monastery of St. Edmundsbury and its system of serfdom as exemplifying the beneficent application of law, order, and godliness by a "real aristocracy." In contrast, early-Victorian England was under the sway of a "sham aristocracy," which seemed to be incapable of preventing the country from tearing itself apart in the class war. In the modern era, it was, for good or ill, the "Captains of Industry" who were the "real aristocracy." Carlyle supported the New Poor Law, because he thought it would "encourage" the "surplus population" to emigrate: "If paupers are made miserable, paupers will needs decline in multitude. It is a secret known to all ratcatchers."[1] Carlyle did not, however, think that it would be sufficient just to inflict more misery on the poor and destitute, and just leave everything to the law of supply and demand. Rather, what was needed was a leader who had the will to impose order in the spirit of 1066. Carlyle, writing in 1850, compares the Norman conquerors to "an immense volunteer police force, stationed everywhere, united, disciplined, feudally regimented, ready for action; strong Teutonic men."[2]

Riding his favorite hobbyhorse of anti-Irish and anti-black bigotry, Carlyle poses the question:

> Between Black West Indians and our own White Ireland, between these two extremes of lazy refusal to work . . . and of inability to find any work, what a world have we made of it, with our fierce mammon-worship, and our benevolent philandering and idle godless nonsense of one kind or another!

As an "alternative," Carlyle calls for a "regiment" of the unemployed to be set to work on the land. Any "responsible" government would tell the "paupers," whether in Ireland, Britain, or the West Indies:

> Refuse to strike into it; shirk the heavy labour, disobey the rules—I will admonish and endeavour to incite you; if in vain, I will flog you; if still in vain, I will at last shoot you—and make God's Earth, and the forlorn-hope in God's Battle, free of you. Understand it I advise you![3]

In 1849, he published an essay attacking American abolitionism, changing the title from *The Negro Question* to *Occasional Discourse on the Nigger Question*, so as to deliberately taunt his opponents. But it also cost him a few friends—most importantly John Stuart Mill, who said in a review for *Frasers Magazine* of Carlyle's idea that some were born to serve others, "a doctrine more damnable . . . never was propounded by a professed moral reformer."

Although Carlyle admired Robert Peel and the Corn Law Repealers for their "heroic" opposition to the ruling sham-aristocracy, he never could accept their underlying liberal philosophy. Carlyle, in his *Latter-Day Pamphlets* of 1850, complains that for liberals Freedom amounts to being "Free, without bond or connection except that of cash payment . . . and law of supply and demand"; worse still, the liberals: "good men, who would stand aghast at the Red Republic and its adjuncts, seem to me to be travelling at full speed towards that or a similar goal!"

The first *Latter-Day Pamphlet*, "The Present Time," begins with an analysis of the European Revolutions of 1848, in which, "Everywhere immeasurable democracy rose monstrous, loud, blatant, inarticulate as the voice of Chaos." The result was that "Although the old histrionic kings will be admitted back under conditions, 'constitutions' with national parliaments. . . . there is no hope that such an arrangement can be made permanent," for they "will be displaced by new explosions occurring more speedily than last time." Carlyle accepts that "universal democracy, whatever we may think of it, has declared itself as an inevitable fact of the days in which we live." And even in England, "though we object to it resolutely in the form of street-barricades and insurrectionary pikes and decidedly will not open doors to it on those terms, the tramp of the million feet is on all streets and thoroughfares, the sound of its bewildered thousand-fold voice is in all writing and speaking, in all thinking and activities of men." The year 1848 in Europe was "a massacre not of the innocents . . . but a universal tumbling of impostors and of impostures into the street." The kings were in fact "Sham-kings, playacting as at Drury Lane" and "what were the people withal that took them for real?" For Carlyle, "the first 'right of man,' compared with which all other rights are as nothing," was "the everlasting privilege of the foolish to be governed by the wise."

As for what democracy actually meant in practice, Carlyle writes:

> Of ancient Republics, and *Demoi*, and Populi, . . . the mass of the population were slaves and the voters intrinsically a kind of Kings, or men born to rule others. . . . [They] were very far from Red Republicans in any political faith whatever!

Carlyle's pamphlet was reviewed by Helen Macfarlane in Harney's *Democratic Review* in a three-part article (the only one written under her real name) titled "Democracy: Remarks on the Times, Apropos of Certain Passages in No. 1 of Thomas Carlyle's

'Latter-Day' Pamphlet." Macfarlane, in her critique of Carlyle, writes:

> One cannot apply any *past* form of experience, as the measure of a *new* thought, without getting involved in endless absurdity. The idea predominant in this pamphlet, and which, I think, pervades all Mr. Carlyle's works, is that of hero-worship.

His great fault is to concentrate on "one aspect of the truth, to the exclusion of all other aspects of the same." Carlyle's "'government, by the best and noblest,' . . . however true this idea may be," is "pushed by him to extremity of denying the rights of personality—of individual man." Carlyle fails to recognize:

> Masses of men can never be *coerced* into the acknowledgement of truth, or into taking steps towards the realisation of an idea. You must *show* them that a thing is true, and good to be done, then they will follow you, willingly as a god-given leader and guide. No man ever governed a country, by the will of its own people, how *expressed* matters not, unless he were the organ chosen by the spirit of the age, the exponent of the Idea which governed that particular epoch, manifesting itself in the whole civilisation of that people.

Democracy, Macfarlane argues, was a "soul in want of a body . . . still seeking an adequate mode of expression," but "rapidly tending towards a realisation in the phenomenal world"; if "the governors stand in direct opposition to the spirit of their age," then "we have an epoch of disorganisation and revolution." In such an epoch, it was historic figures such as Auguste Blanqui who expressed the will of the people and invoked "the spirit of the age." Elsewhere in her writings, Macfarlane sometimes slips in phrases and concepts of Blanqui's. One of them, "Republic without Helots," comes from Blanqui's speech to the French court in 1849, in which he explains the difference between his own insurrectionary role in 1848 and the "heroism" of an older "real aristocracy." The speech was translated and published in Harney's paper:

It is said, labour, currency, and credit are affairs of political economy and not of feeling. I know not, but faith and enthusiasm are lovers to move the world from its foundations. Let us begin there, the rest will follow. Alexander, in the desert of Gedrosia, scattered on the sand some water that was brought to him in a helmet, exclaiming, 'Every one, or no one!' The self-denial of the General electrified the dispirited Macedonian army and saved it by inspiring courage and hope. When the people are starving, no one ought to eat. This is my utopia, my dream in the February Days. It raised up against me the heat of implacable enemies. I wished to touch the consciences of men; they only thought of letting loose conflicting class interests. Yet the question was not that of a Republic of Spartans, but of a Republic without Helots. Perhaps my utopia will appear the most absurd and the most impossible of all. Then may God have mercy on France![4]

In Macfarlane's view, the counterrevolutionary role of the bourgeoisie in Europe had proved that "coercion is the necessary condition for the existence of these 'sham-governors.'. . . . representatives of the ghosts of old, dead, formulas . . . who ought to be kicked indefinitely into infinite space—beyond creation, if that were practicable." Carlyle's "artistic temperament" could not "endure the ruin and decay to which society in Europe" was "fast hastening."

Engels, in an essay for the *Revue der Neuen Rheinischen Zeitung* in 1843, describes Carlyle's writings as a striking illustration of "how a noble, knowing and wise man in practice becomes a cad, an ignoramus and a fool."[5] The critique of "Feudal Socialism" in *The Communist Manifesto* seems to be directed at Carlyle (it doesn't actually name him) more than anyone else. In Macfarlane's translation, the *Manifesto* argues that, since the aristocracy was no longer capable, after 1830, of waging a serious political struggle against the bourgeoisie, there "remained only the possibility of conducting a literary combat"; of hurling "lampoons and fearful prophecies of coming woe," as "advocates" for the industrial proletariat. But the "feudalists," who liked to point out that the modern proletariat never existed under their rule, ignored the fact that they themselves had created the bourgeoisie. They reproached the bourgeoisie for creating the proletariat, but because the idea of proletarian revolution was their greatest fear of all, they supported all the reactionary measures the bourgeoisie employed to deal with unrest and revolt.

America

Macfarlane points out that Carlyle accepts democracy as "the fact of the present age," but denies its existence in past or present. Macfarlane agrees and adds: "Not even in America?—asks a reader. I answer, decidedly not."

Carlyle writes on the "Republic of United States":

> Their quality of cotton dollars, industry and resources I believe to be almost unspeakable; but I can by no means worship the likes of these. . . . what great thought, what great noble thing, that one could worship, or loyally admire has yet been produced there? None . . . "What have they done," growls Smellfungus ". . . they have begotten, with rapidity beyond recorded example, Eighteen Million of the greatest bores ever seen in this world."

Macfarlane's critique of the American Republic is more serious, pointing out that in the "middle-class view":

> European society, with its vicious organization of labour, is to be transported en masse to new countries and the world will be saved . . . the middle-class system of production and distribution, which has occasioned evils now fast becoming intolerable in the old world, is making itself felt in the new one also.

She adds, borrowing a point made in *The Communist Manifesto*, that "The agrarian reformers there, however, are taking the bull by the horns—they are boldly grappling the land question." The National Reform Association, founded in America in 1845 by George Henry Evans, publisher of the *Working Mans Advocate*, stood for the ten-hour day, land-nationalization, suppression of profiteering, and abolition of slavery—though by the end of the 1840s the movement was in fact petering out.[6]

Macfarlane's critique of the United States of America centers on the issues of race and sex:

> There are two facts existing in that country—to me they are very disgusting facts—which are opposed to the democratic idea, as any institution in the old world. American negro slavery, and American exclusion of white women from the exercises of all political, and many social rights—are things as much opposed to freedom and fraternity, as Russian serfdom, Austrian military despotism and English class legislation.

In "The Red Flag in 1850," Macfarlane expounds further on the limits of merely political reforms in reference to the actually existing republic of the United States:

> In America, women generally and coloured people are enslaved and used up by the free and enlightened citizens of that sham republic . . . the same causes must ultimately produce the same effects . . . irresponsible power has been shifted from one class to another; in one country its possession depends on the accidents of birth and wealth; in another on those of colour and sex."[7]

The feminist movement in America came into existence when white women campaigning against slavery drew inspiration from black abolitionists such as Sojourner Truth and decided to fight for their own freedom as well. The most revolutionary event of 1848 in America had been the Women's Rights Convention at Seneca Falls, New York. At the time Macfarlane was writing, this movement was still active and organizing for a second convention in 1851.

The Most Joyful of All Spectacles

Carlyle's view of the world, according to Engels, could be deduced from

> on the one hand, vestiges of Tory romanticism and humane attitudes originating with Goethe, and, on the other, sceptical,

empirical England. . . . Carlyle's dualism is aggravated by the fact that though he is acquainted with German literature, he is not acquainted with its necessary corollary, German philosophy.[8]

In Macfarlane's analysis, formed out of her familiarity with German philosophy, democracy had assumed four historical forms: "the religion taught by the divine Galilean Republican"; the Medieval heretics and the Reformation; the "German philosophy from Immanuel Kant to Hegel"; and the "democracy of our own times," in which "faith has been transfigured into knowledge," now "divested of the opaque element of empiricism."

> M. Carlyle qualifies Red Republicanism—i.e., the Democracy, which he admits is the fact of the nineteenth century, by the epithet "mere inarticulate bellowing." This reminds me of the old saying, "he that hath ears, let him hear what the Spirit saith to the churches. " Red Republicanism is just about one of the most articulate, plain speaking voices, in the whole of Universal History. I opine it is not very difficult to reach the true meaning of this fact, but we must study it in the light of eighteen centuries of Christianity, or what has hitherto passed for such.

Referring to her own experience of the 1848 Revolutions (in the one article she mentions it), Macfarlane writes:

> I am free to confess that, for me the most joyful of all spectacles possible in these times is the one which Mr. Carlyle laments; one which I enjoyed extremely at Vienna, in March 1848—i.e., "an universal tumbling of impostors." For it amounts to this, that men are determined to live no longer in lies. . . . *Ca ira*! And how do men come to perceive that the old social forms are worn out and useless? By the advent of a new Idea. . . . We may safely predict that the Democratic Idea will survive the butcheries of a Haynau.

The 1848 Revolutions, according to Macfarlane, were the expression of an epoch in which universal reason has reached such a degree of development in individual man that, when the thought, the fact, of the epoch, is presented to society, it is seen to be true. As for the adherents of the old system, they attempt to enforce order by means of coercion. . . . but the idea is a subtle thing and eludes their grasp.

Democracy was "the nightmare and 'old bogy' of all respectable formalists," who always ask, "'what will people say of it?' Not, 'is it true? Is it right?'" "For choice," writes Macfarlane, "I would rather be an architect than a scavenger; it is better to build up than to pull down and sweep away. Yet the scavenger is a very useful kind of person. So is the destructive, the go-ahead radical of the present day."[9]

Notes

1. Thomas Carlyle, *Critical and Miscellaneous Essays IV* (London: Chapman Hall,1872), 130.

2. Carlyle, *Essays IV*, 189.

3. Thomas Carlyle, *The Latter-Day Pamphlets* (London: Chapman and Hall, 1850), 1–50.

4. Blanqui's speech was published in the *Friend of the People*, July 26, 1851.

5. Friedrich Engels, *The Condition of England*, in Marx and Engels, *Collected Works Vol. 3*, 444–68.

6. Hal Draper, *The Adventures of the Communist Manifesto* (Berkeley: Centre for Socialist History, 1994), 315.

7. *Red Republican*, July 13, 1850.

8. Engels, *Condition of England*.

9. *Democratic Review*, April 1850.

11

The Translation of
The Communist Manifesto

> The *Manifesto* is remarkable for its imaginative power,
> its expression and grasp of the luminous and dreadful
> possibilities that pervade modern life. Along with
> everything else that it is, it is the first great modernist
> work of art.
>
> —Marshall Berman,
> *All That Is Solid Melts into Air*

The Communist Manifesto of 1848 originated in the coming together of two currents in the German Emigration. Firstly, there
was the "artisan-communism" of the "League of the Just." Set
up as a "secret society" in Paris, in 1836, the League participated
in Blanqui's failed uprising of 1840, after which, its "central authority" moved from Paris to London. The League set up German Workers Educational Associations in Switzerland, England,
Belgium, the United States, and France. According to Marx, the
League's "democratic constitution [was] completely at variance
with the purposes of a conspiratorial society" and its organizational form was "at least not disconsonant with the tasks of a
propaganda society." Marx says that the "doctrine" of the
League "underwent all the transformations of French and English socialism, as well as the German varieties," and that "the
various phases that German philosophy underwent between

1839 and 1846 were followed with eager partizanship in the bosom of the workers' societies."[1]

A second current of communism came about as a result of Marx's move to Paris in 1843. Marx explains that in Paris he "cultivated personal relations with the leader of the League of the Just [Karl Schapper] there, as I did the leaders of most of the French workers' societies, without however joining any of these." When Marx was expelled from France in 1847, he and Engels set up a German Workers Educational Association in Brussels and formed an international "Communist Correspondence Committee." In 1847 the League of the Just leadership in London broke with the utopian ideas of their founder, Wilhelm Weitling, and changed the name to the "Communist League." As the membership as a whole had become interested in the new ideas of "critical communism," the central authority sent watchmaker Joseph Moll to Brussels to discuss collaboration with Marx and Engels.[2]

Marx and Engels still had serious misgivings about the conspiratorial tradition of oaths and rituals that the League still practiced, but Moll persuaded them that, with Weitling decamped to New York, they could contribute "toward replacing the League's obsolete organisation with a new one befitting our times and aims." In June 1847 League members from Switzerland, Belgium, France, Germany, and England met at a secret congress in London and voted to democratize the organization and circulate a "Communist Credo" for discussion with all interested parties. Engels, who attended it (Marx could not make the trip), was delegated to draft the document. In the months following, Engels suggested to Marx that since "a certain amount of history had to be related in it," the present "catechism" form was no longer suitable and a "communist manifesto" would be much more effective. In November 1847, in preparation for another congress in London, Engels, "in frightful haste," sketched out the "Principles of Communism" and wrote to Marx: "I begin: What is communism? And then right on to the proletariat—history of its genesis, difference from earlier workers, development of the opposition of proletariat and bourgeoisie, crises, consequences."[3] The December 1847 congress of the League unanimously approved the "principles" and commissioned Marx and Engels to write *The Communist Manifesto*. At this point Engels handed the project over to Marx, who, under great pressure from the League to finish it quickly, wrote it up without further consultation with Engels.[4]

Three weeks into February 1848, a thousand copies were printed in German type by the League supporter Burghard for the cost of five pounds. Its dark green cover bore the words, which translated into English, read:

> *Manifesto of the Communist Party*. Published in February 1848—Proletarians of all countries, unite!—London. Printed in the offices of the "Educational Society for Workers" by J. E. Burghard. 46, Liverpool Street, Bishopsgate.

A question arises: if the *Manifesto* was issued by the Communist League, a German organization, then why did it announce itself as the manifesto of the Communist *Party*, calling on "Proletarians of all countries" to unite? Draper points out that "at this time, well before the development of the modern party systems in politics, the word 'party' (in any European language) meant primarily a tendency or current of opinion, not an organized group." The title of the *Manifesto* reflected "an attitude looking away from sectism"; it was "an advance notice of the de-emphasis of the sect," presented "on behalf of a broader current of politics than was contained within the organizational walls of any league."[5]

This "broader current" included, of course, Chartism, and in particular Harney, whose input to the thinking of the *Manifesto* was crucial. Indeed, it could be argued that the conditions in England in 1847, marked by a period of capitalist crisis that had prevailed since the early 1840s, fitted the perspective of *Manifesto* more than anywhere else. As pointed out in chapter 4, the Fraternal Democrats did not counterpose themselves to the Chartists as a "party" to lead. As Rothstein puts it: "The reasons which at first prompted the Fraternal Democrats to reject all forms of party organisation are worthy of note, for precisely at that moment Marx and Engels were penning the opening lines of the second chapter of the Communist manifesto, which also declared that Communists did not form any separate party."[6]

The ink had hardly dried on the *Manifesto* when the Revolution broke out in Paris and thence rapidly engulfed most of Europe. During the spring of 1848 the *Manifesto* was reprinted three times and serialized in the *Deutsche London Zeitung*. The statement in the preamble of the *Manifesto*, that it was to be translated into English, French, Italian, Flemish, and Danish, soon proved, however, to be overoptimistic. In December 1848 a Swedish translation did appear in Stockholm, but the next translation would be the English one by Helen Macfarlane, two years later.

The Macfarlane Translation

Described by Harney as the "most revolutionary document ever given to the world," the English translation of *The Communist Manifesto* was serialized in the *Red Republican* in the four issues beginning November 9, 1850. Harney states, in his introduction to this "excellent translation," that the original "was drawn up in January 1848, by Citizens Charles Marx and Frederic Engels." This was the first public statement anywhere of the authorship of the *Manifesto*. No credit appeared for the translation, however, and not until 1872 was it publicly revealed, by Marx and Engels in their preface to the German edition of the *Manifesto*, that it "was published in the English for first time in 1850 in the *Red Republican*, translated by Miss Helen Macfarlane."

In the *Red Republican* translation there are some significant alterations to the text. Firstly, the original title, *Manifesto of the Communist Party*, becomes *German Communism: Manifesto of the German Communist Party*. Thus the word "German" is inserted into the title twice over, which somewhat de-emphasizes its internationalist thrust, as does the removal of a sentence from the *Manifesto*'s short introduction, announcing that "Communists of various nationalities have assembled in

London, and sketched the following manifesto, to be published in the English, French, German, Italian, Flemish and Danish languages." Thirdly, the first chapter heading, "Bourgeois and Proletarians," is missing, as is the first sentence of the chapter: "The history of all hitherto existing society is the history of class struggles." (Samuel Moore translation.) This is a surprising omission, since in her own writings, as we have already seen, Macfarlane puts great importance on this insight: "From the earliest dawn of civilization . . . we see nothing else going on than the struggles between classes or castes. . . . It has continued to be an historical fact down to our own times . . . the battles of social castes form the narrative of history."[7] Fourthly, part of the section on "Position of the Communists in Relation to the Various Existing Opposition Parties"—some three hundred words—is missing. In the original this text comes directly after the section heading (which is also omitted). In Moore's translation, it reads:

> The Communists fight for the attainment of the immediate aims, for the enforcement of the momentary interests of the working-class; but in the movement of the present, they also represent and take care of the future of that movement. In France, the Communists ally with the Social Democrats against the conservative and radical bourgeoisie, reserving, however, the right to take up a critical position in regard to phases and illusions traditionally handed down from the Great Revolution.
>
> In Switzerland, they support the Radicals, without losing sight of the fact that this party consists of antagonistic elements, partly of Democratic Socialists, in the French sense, partly of radical bourgeois.
>
> In Poland, they support the party that insists on an agrarian revolution as the prime condition for national emancipation, that party which fomented the insurrection of Krakow in 1846.
>
> In Germany, they fight with the bourgeoisie whenever it acts in a revolutionary way, against the absolute monarchy, the feudal squirearchy, and the petty-bourgeoisie.
>
> But they never cease, for a single instant, to instill into the working-class the clearest possible recognition of the hostile

antagonism between bourgeoisie and proletariat, in order that the German workers may straightway use, as so many weapons against the bourgeoisie, the social and political conditions that the bourgeoisie must necessarily introduce along with its supremacy, and in order that, after the fall of the reactionary classes in Germany, the fight against the bourgeoisie itself may immediately begin.

The Communists turn their attention chiefly to Germany, because that country is on the eve of a bourgeois revolution that is bound to be carried out under more advanced conditions of European civilization and with a much more developed proletariat than that of England was in the seventeenth, and France in the eighteenth century, and because the bourgeois revolution in Germany will be but the prelude to an immediately following proletarian revolution.

It is unlikely that this was omitted at the suggestion of Marx and Engels, since in all subsequent editions and translations it was left in; and there is no evidence that they agreed to any request by Harney to leave it out. There is no footnote by Macfarlane explaining the omission and it seems unlikely that she made the cut without consulting the authors. It seems likely then, that Harney, as editor, was responsible for all of the above changes, which had the effect of playing down the internationalist perspective of the *Manifesto*. With the new Aliens Act in force, Harney, the most internationalist of all Chartist leaders, had reason to be wary of alerting the government to anything that might seen as a "conspiracy" hatched in London between "aliens" and Chartists. He had, after all, been having talks during the year 1850 with the German Communists and French Blanquists about a prospective "World League of Revolutionary Socialists."

The chapter and subchapter headings in Macfarlane's translation of *The Communist Manifesto* are almost the same as Moore's in 1888: "Bourgeois and Proletarians"; "Proletarians and Communists"; "Reactionary Socialism (Feudal Socialism, Petit-Bourgeois Socialism, German or 'True' Socialism)"; "Conservative, or Bourgeois Socialism"; "Critical-Utopian Socialism and Communism." Macfarlane differs, however, in using the term "Shopocrat Socialism" where Moore later uses "Petit-Bourgeois Socialism." Macfarlane explains in a footnote:

> The term in the original is *Kleinburger*; meaning small burghers, or citizens. A class, comprising small capitalists generally, whether small-farmers, small-manufacturers, or retail shopkeepers. As these last form the predominant element of this class in England, I have chosen the word *Shopocrat* to express the German term.

"Shopocrat" had been in use in Chartist circles since the 1830s. In using it in the *Manifesto*, Macfarlane was attempting to boost the radical Chartist critique of the cooperative retail movement, which the Christian Socialists were pushing as an alternative to political mobilization for the Charter.

The opening sentence of the *Manifesto* ("*Ein Gespenst geht um in Europa—des Gespenst des Kommunismus*") is rendered in the 1888 translation as "A spectre is haunting Europe. The spectre of Communism." Macfarlane's translation of the opening sentence is more exotic: "A frightful hobgoblin stalks throughout Europe. We are haunted by a ghost. The ghost of Communism."

Macfarlane tries to give *Ein Gespenst* a double meaning. It is not just the ghostly apparition that haunts the castles of Shakespeare's Macbeth and Hamlet, foretelling doom and retribution for the incumbents. It is also the scary sprite that country folks tell their children lurks in the woods, in order to discourage them from wandering off on their own. Draper cites three articles published in the German press in the years preceding 1848 that refer to "communism" as a "spectre." As Oscar Hammens puts it: "When Marx spoke of a 'spectre of communism' haunting Europe in 1848, he was stating a verifiable fact, as far as France and the German world were concerned."[8]

While Macfarlane's use of "hobgoblin" rather than "spectre" is certainly questionable, even unfortunate, her translation for the most part is a powerful statement. The most potent images in the *Manifesto* lose none of their strength in her translation.[9] In further "adventures" of the "spectre," in the section where Marx and Engels give the image a Faustian twist, Moore renders it as:

Modern bourgeois society with its relations of production, of exchange and of property, a society that has conjured up such gigantic means of production and of exchange, is like the sorcerer, who is no longer able to control the powers of the nether world who he has called up by his spells.

In Macfarlane we get:

Modern middle-class society, which has revolutionized the conditions of property, and called forth such colossal means of production and traffic, resembles the wizard who evoked the powers of darkness, but could neither master them, nor yet get rid of them when they had come at his bidding.

Moore's translation of another celebrated passage goes:

Constant Revolutions of production, uninterrupted disturbance of all social conditions, everlasting uncertainty and agitation distinguish the bourgeois epoch from all earlier ones. All fixed, fast frozen relations, with their train of ancient and venerable prejudices and opinions are swept away, all new-formed ones become antiquated before they can ossify. All that is solid melts into air, all that is holy is profaned, and man is at last compelled to face with sober senses, his real conditions of life, and his relations with his kind.

Marshall Berman, in his study of modernism, *All That Is Solid Melts into Air*, suggests that the above paragraph "is more complex and more interesting than the standard nineteenth-century assertion that God does not exist. Marx is moving in the dimension of time, working to evoke an ongoing historical drama and trauma. He is saying that the aura of holiness is suddenly missing, and that we cannot understand ourselves until we confront what is absent."[10]

The Macfarlane translation of the same paragraph reads:

A continual change in the modes of production, a never ceasing state of agitation and social insecurity, distinguish the Bourgeois-Epoch from all preceding ones. The ancient ties between men, their opinions and beliefs—hoar with antiquity—are fast disappearing, and new ones become worn out ere they can become firmly rooted. Everything fixed and stable vanishes, everything holy and venerable is desecrated, and men are forced to look at their mutual relations, at the problem of life, in the soberest, most matter of fact way.

Although Moore's line "All that is solid melts into air, all that is holy is profaned" is by far the strongest, Macfarlane's rendition of the paragraph tends to reinforce Berman's point: that what is at issue is not just a negative—the "death of God"— but also the "problem of Life," of how to "understand ourselves," a problem that calls for a new affirmation of what it is to be Human.

As soon as the *Manifesto* had been published in the *Red Republican* it aroused sufficient interest for the *Times* to quote some passages to illustrate what the editor regarded as the deplorable state of the "literture [sic] of the poor."[11] Marx decided to seek out a publisher for the translation in America and sent copies of it to Eduard Koch, an exiled revolutionary who worked as journalist on the *New Yorker Staatszeitung*. When Koch failed to respond to the suggestion that he publish the *Manifesto* as a brochure, Marx wrote to another German exile in America, Joseph Weydemeyer, in the hope that he might get Charles Dana, editor of the *New York Daily Tribune*, to put it out. Again nothing came of it.

Two decades later the Macfarlane translation of the *Manifesto* was given a new lease on life when it was reprinted in New York in 1871 in the aftermath of the Paris Commune. At that time there was intense public interest in the ideas of the "German doctor" who led the International Working Men's Association. Firstly, extracts appeared in the *New York World;* then shortly afterward, Victoria Woodhull, the spiritualist, financial schemer, free-thinker, and feminist, decided that publishing this rare document in her paper, *Woodhull and Claflin's Weekly,* would further her aim of taking over the American sections of the International. Woodhull, who was seeking financial support from Cornelius Vanderbilt for her ventures, wanted to turn the International away from working-class struggle toward her own coalition, which seemed to embrace the kind of ideas that a century or so later would be packaged as "New Age." In neither case was Macfarlane credited as the translator.[12]

When Marx died in 1883, a massive memorial meeting was held at the Cooper Union in New York. Johann Most, a German émigré anarchist who published the paper *Freiheit* in New York, told the gathering: "When I saw Marx for the last time, . . . he said to me: 'I will not see the triumph of our cause, but you are young enough.'" According to the historian Sheldon P. Foner: "His assertion left the impression with the audience that Marx's writings were part of the foundations of anarchism." Most then hijacked a project launched by the memorial committee to republish the Macfarlane translation in America and used the committee funds to publish under the name of his own sect. Also, without consulting the *Manifesto*'s surviving coauthor, Engels, Most took the liberty of deleting some of its passages, such as the ten-point program in Section II. A so-called "translators footnote"—Macfarlane yet again wasn't credited—stated that the ten points were "not applicable at the present time, as more radical measures are necessary."[13]

After 1888, the Samuel Moore translation of the *Manifesto*, which was done in collaboration with Engels, superseded the Macfarlane version in the English-speaking world.

Notes

1. Karl Marx, *Herr Vogt* (London: New Park, 1982), 60.
2. Marx, *Herr Vogt*, 60–61.
3. Engels to Marx, November 23, 1847, in Marx and Engels, *Collected Works Vol. 27*, 107.
4. Hal Draper, *The Adventures of the Communist Manifesto* (Berkeley: Centre for Socialist History, 1994), 11.
5. Draper, *Adventures*, 13–15.
6. Rothstein, *From Chartism to Labourism*, 13–15.
7. *Democratic Review*, September 1850.
8. Draper, *Adventures*, 194–95.
9. The 1888 English translation of the *Manifesto* by Samuel Moore was commissioned by Engels.

10. Marshall Berman, *All That is Solid Melts into Air: The Experience of Modernity* (London: Verso 1983), 89.

11. Draper, *Adventures*, 30. *The Times*, London, September 2, 1871.

12. Draper, *Adventures*, 45.

13. Draper, *Adventures*, 66–68.

12

Theory and Organization

A "Double Movement"

When, in mid-1850, the Fraternal Democrats won a majority on the executive of the National Charter Association, Harney decided that the time had come to transform the N.C.A. into a new "socialist-democratic party." Harney got the N.C.A. to convene a series of conferences, beginning in August 1850 and running into the following year, which involved Owenite cooperators, Christian socialists, George Holyoake's Social Reformers, Bronterre O'Brien's National Reform League, and the Metropolitan Trades Council. The problem with this initiative was that all of the invited participants had their own agendas and feared losing their political identities in an organization dominated by the N.C.A. and its Fraternal Democrat–Red Republican leadership.[1] Helen Macfarlane, in an article entitled "Democratic Organisation," tried to convince them of the soundness of Harney's perspective.

Macfarlane, as we have seen, complained of religious sects whose creeds rise up "like a wall between the unhappy sectarians and the rest of the universe; beyond which it is forbidden to look on pain of damnation, or worse." In the sense that all sectarians possess a "doctrine," and follow an infallible (or "correct") interpretation (or interpretor) of it, her words could equally apply to some of the radical parties in her time (and indeed all times

since). At Chartist meeting halls, artisans schooled in classical political economy, who advocated "a fair days work for a fair days
pay," would fight it out with proletarian communists who
wanted to completely abolish "wage slavery"; O'Connorite advocates of the smallholder Land Plan would be denounced for
would-be landlordism by Spencean advocates of wholesale land
nationalization; Christian-Socialist cooperators who wanted to be
left alone to cooperate would be accused of abandoning the class
struggle by Chartist "physical forcers," etc. Entering into this
melee, Macfarlane's polemical style is punchy enough, but her
method is "Hegelian": in the sense of attempting find common
ground with the "opposition" and getting "inside" their essential
concepts, so as to move them forward toward a new dialectical
unity of principles. For example, in challenging Holyoake's Social Reformers (who stood for moral-force Chartism, Freethink-
ing, and Cooperation) on the question of "rights," Macfarlane
argues that posing the question of any right cannot ignore the reality of a society that "does not give me the power of exercising
it." For Macfarlane, talk about "rights" only becomes meaningful
when it addresses "principles":

> I take it for granted that all sections of Social Reformers are
> agreed on the necessity of a radical change in the existing sys-
> tem of unlimited competition. . . . But a radical change can only
> be effected by substituting the principle of Association for that
> of Competition.[2]

Beginning from this "principle of Association," Macfarlane
draws the two propositions that "soil and capital are collective
property" and "that these instruments of labour being common
to All, should be used to the benefit of All . . . on the principles
of Association and Universal Solidarity." These are equivalent to
two of the ten measures advocated in *The Communist Manifesto*;
but here, she suggests, they are "propositions resulting from the
natural and inalienable Rights of Man, and are common ground
upon which all sections of Social Reformers can meet." Macfarlane goes on to say that "many important consequences" are
"derivable from these two fundamental propositions." She mod-

estly qualifies her observations by saying "my limits do not allow me to enter" into these consequences "which have been fully developed in the works of the Continental Socialists," but then shows how much she has taken up Marx's proviso in *The Communist Manifesto* that measures "will of course, be different in different countries." Macfarlane suggests seven measures "for example" (numbers added in brackets):

[1] Education is gratuitous and obligatory.
[2] Justice is administered gratuitously.
[3] The State supports such citizens as are incapable of work, through old age or disease, and this support is not a *charity*, it is a *right*.
[4] Private banks are to be abolished, and replaced by a single national bank.
[5] Indirect taxation is to be abolished and succeeded by a single direct tax.
[6] Usury will be abolished, and replaced by a system of gratuitous national credit.
[7] Paper will be substituted for the present metallic currency, and so forth.

In fact, points 1, 2, 3, and 7—concerning education, justice, social welfare, and currency—were realized, to a greater or lesser extent, in Britain within a hundred years. In the case of the three measures that weren't (bank nationalization, abolition of indirect taxation, and universal access to free credit—which are also "in line" with *The Communist Manifesto*) there is of course, from the standpoint of the twenty-first century good cause for wishing they had been, considering the oppressive globalized power of finance-capital, the role of indirect taxes in transferring the tax burden from the rich to the poor, and a Third World starved by debt.

Centralization

On receiving a challenge from a group of Welsh supporters of the *Red Republican* to expound on the objective of the "socialist" tendency, Macfarlane responds with a call for the "centralization" of "Democratic interests," represented by the N.C.A., the Reform League, Owenites, etc. To "the followers of Owen," Macfarlane puts the question: "Why is it, that with all their expenditure of time and money, they have never been able to put any of their Social theories into practice?" Her answer is that "The battle between the classes composing society must be fought out first." Taking an organizational position identical to Blanqui's in France, she argues for a centralized movement, led from the capital. This had as much to do with the divisions between Northern England and the South as between the nationalities of England, Wales, Scotland, and Ireland. In the case of Ireland, she sees British oppression there as akin to the subjugation of nationalities in the Hapsburg Empire: "How long would it be before the Hungarians, Italians, Croats and Poles would assert their independence, and the Viennese people plant the red flag on the dome of St. Stephen?," should the Hapsburgs "disband any portion of their colossal standing army?" The answer—not long—is also applied to the British government:

> Let them withdraw their garrisons from the financial districts, and from Ireland,—let them disband their constables and dismiss their police spies—and the "glorious British constitution" would not survive this suicidal policy a single week.

Against the "political and social quacks" of the Malthusian school, who propounded emigration as a remedy to poverty, she insists that the conditions of the Irish peasantry would not be improved "until there has been a social revolution in that country" and that there would be no freedom "until the rose, the shamrock, and the thistle, be woven into one wreath for the altar of Liberty; not until the Saxon and Celt—forgetting all their senseless feuds and animosities—rally round the Red Banner to the battle cry of the new epoch, *Vive la République, Democratique et Sociale!*"[3]

The affairs of Scottish Chartism are absent from Macfarlane's writings, although this is not surprising, considering that Chartist activity in Scotland had been at a low ebb since the repression of radicalism by the Scottish authorities in the early 1840s. (What there was of Chartism north of the border was largely independent of the English Chartist organizations, although the Fraternal Democrats had a presence in some areas.) Macfarlane was aware that Scotland suffered poverty on a scale closer to Ireland than England: "In England about one in twelve of the population—in Scotland, one in nine—in Ireland one in eight—are paupers." And in judging the "state church in Scotland" and "dissenters generally" to be just as "pagan" as the church of Rome or England, she nevertheless allows that the former had accumulated less wealth for themselves at the expense of their congregations and that "certain striking deviations from the Christian principle of equality and fraternity are not so rife."[4]

Alisdair MacIntyre's study of the Scottish Enlightenment shows how the mix of Aristotelian philosophy and Calvinist theology in the Scottish universities in the seventeenth and early eighteenth centuries produced a notion of the "Good Society," in which the basic unit was the household of the smallholding farmer, watched over by an authority that upheld definite social, moral, and theological principles. After the Act of Union, this peculiarly Scottish notion of a "moral economy" was challenged by the new Anglicizing liberalism of David Hume. For Hume, the basic unit of society was the acquisitive individual; and land, like everything else, was a commodity and fair game for enclosing capitalists. After the Civil Wars of the seventeenth century, the English bourgeoisie had had enough of arguments over how "higher" principles should govern the "natural" (capitalist) order of society, which had now become a mass of competing passions and needs, all functioning through transactions and exchanges. What was needed was a social structure to preserve order rather than redress incurable inequalities; and this structure, Hume maintained, was essentially what had been established in England by "Dutch William's" invasion of 1688.[5]

Nevertheless, the Aristotelian-Calvinist philosophic tradition lived on as an element of Scottish radical dissent. Walter Kendall, writing on the question of why twentieth-century

Marxism found more a fertile soil in Scotland than in England, says:

> Religion, the ideology of the establishment in Britain, had in Scotland a more striking record of national struggle. Penetrating deeper into the culture of the people, it gave them a penchant for the cut and thrust of logical argument, an appreciation and enthusiasm for dialectics not to be found in England.[6]

It is then perhaps no accident that *The Communist Manifesto* was first translated by a Scot; one who, like the Scottish Jacobins of an earlier generation, looked to France rather than England for political inspiration. In calling for the organizational unity of the forces of "social propaganda" and "democratic agitation," Macfarlane sees in Chartist organizational practice an Anglo-Saxon "tradition" lacking the effectiveness of the French, as represented by the Blanquists:

> How comes it that our French brothers have done so much compared with us? Because they are organized into one compact mass, which, under the guidance of competent leaders, moves like an army of well-disciplined soldiers, steadily onward to a given point. That is the reason of it. Frenchmen have the instinct of military discipline. We, on the other hand, carry the Saxon principle of the local management and the infinitesimal division of interests, too far. Absolutely this will not do in fighting a battle.

Blanqui and Marx

There was much more to August Blanqui, who spent a total of thirty-five years as a political prisoner, than his vast reserves of revolutionary will and the dedication and loyalty of his supporters.

Blanqui was hostile to the faddish but influential sociological doctrine of positivism as espoused by Comte, who advocated a new caste system of intellectuals and industrialists to help "inoculate" the masses against socialism and revolution. In contrast, Blanqui's politics represented the objective experience of the French proletariat who, from the July Revolution of 1830 to the Commune of 1871, found it impossible to compromise with a bourgeoisie that had few scruples about using violence in the class war. The French workers had to learn the necessity of meeting repression with an effective strategy for conditions of illegality. There was then, a real unity between Blanqui's thought, for all its eclecticism and rootedness in eighteenth-century materialism, and his political practice. Blanqui saw Reason as the motive power of reality and its triumph as depending on how successfully the mind purged itself of all mysticism, dogma, and superstition. Blanqui upheld the eighteenth-century French materialism of Hollbach, Voltaire, and Rousseau as the rightful inheritance of the proletariat, as what gave the proletarian body its head. For Blanqui, the idea that humanity's liberty, well-being, and strivings for "perfection" were rooted in science and the progress of history was what provided the space in his mind to conquer the torments of his prisons with the "faith and enthusiasm . . . to move the world from its foundations."

Walter Benjamin says of Blanqui:

> It is hardly possible to overestimate the revolutionary prestige Blanqui had at the time of his death. Before Lenin there was no one else with a clearer profile of the Proletariat.[7]

Blanqui was convinced that an organization formed to replace capitalist rule with a "Revolutionary Dictatorship" required a method as scientific as that of a surgeon curing a patient, and a discipline, if not a certain fanaticism, suitable for preparing an insurrection. Blanqui's approach manifested itself in the organizations he founded: secret societies whose very names—the Society of Families and Society of Seasons—reflected a "natural" hierarchical order. In the Seasons, for example, cadres called "Sundays" were assigned to organize units of six rank-and-file members who were each named after the other days of the week; the Sundays were led by higher-ups called "Julys"; and so on up the pyramid of command. However, in periods when representative democracy, right of assembly, and freedom of speech were holding sway, as in the first half of 1848, Blanqui abandoned secret organizational methods and advocated the unity of all the republican and socialist clubs. According to Sam Bernstein, Marx, during his short stay in Paris in spring 1848, joined the Society of the Rights of Man, which had thirty-four thousand members on its Paris membership roll. Marx argued within for a campaign of all-out propaganda, an alliance of the democratic clubs, the arming of the workers in the National Guard, and the postponement of the general elections. (The elections, which were largely rigged, did take place, and Bonaparte's landslide victory doomed the Second Republic.)

In Engels's posthumous assessment of Blanqui, he was "a political revolutionary in essence and a socialist in sentiment only . . . but devoid of socialist theory and of positive, practical proposals for social redress." Blanqui, however, saw how easily the bourgeois "republic without republicans" of 1848 had disabled that exponent of "socialist theory," Louis Blanc, by taking him at his word on the power of reason, fraternity, and altruism. The bourgeois regime had made Blanc the official theorist of the "Labour Commission," a talking shop set up to deflect workers' demands for a Ministry of Labour with real powers to assist the establishment of cooperative workshops. Blanqui wasn't against theory; he thought the more theories the merrier. Wasn't that what democracy was all about? He was no admirer of Robespierre, who had betrayed materialist reason of the French Revolution with his cult of the "supreme being." Blanqui, however, was not immune to French chauvinism. The one German thinker to grab his attention was Marx, who tirelessly campaigned for his freedom whenever it was denied him. Though never a Marxist, Blanqui appreciated Marx's critique of Proudhon, whose "socialism" amounted to a plan to establish a credit bank for small producers, to enable them to take on the capitalist competitors on an "equal" basis.

In 1861, Marx wrote to Blanqui, "No one could be more interested than I in the fate of a man who I always regarded as the head and heart of the proletarian party in France." Indeed, Marx's projection in 1850 of the "Revolution in Permanence" seems to take off from Blanqui's conception of democracy as a dynamic revolutionary process. After 1848, Blanqui broke from Armand Barbes's vision of democracy as a formal structure to be set up for the purpose of eliminating the dynamics of social discord and creating a static "equilibrium" based on "fraternity *between* the classes." As Bernstein puts it, Blanqui rejected this positivism because he:

> thought of democracy as a process, with a history and a future. In practice it meant a series of acts which climaxed in what was then designated as the social republic. And being a process, it could neither ignore the past nor be mummified like revolutionary relics. . . . democracy, from Blanqui's viewpoint, had to become socialism, or it would be nothing more than a convenient cover for any one, even for its enemies when they desire to disguise their intentions.[8]

Right up to Blanqui's death in 1881, Marx never ceased to try and open up a dialogue with him and his organization. The differences between them, however, should not be underestimated. Marx saw Blanqui's concept of "Revolutionary Dictatorship" as dangerously abstract—hence the need for a content, as projected in Marx's preferred term: the "Revolutionary Dictatorship of the *Proletariat*" [emphasis mine]. The term "dictatorship" had much less emotive connotations than later became the case in the era of Hitler and Stalin. From the Jacobin dictatorship of 1793 to the revolutionary and counter-revolutionary regimes of 1848 to 1851, nearly all governments came to power through the violent—dictatorial—overthrow of the existing order. Marx, writing in 1850 on the lessons of 1848, argues that for the revolutionary workers:

> Socialism is the declaration of the permanence of the revolution, the class dictatorship of the proletariat as the necessary transit point to the abolition of class distinctions generally, to the abolition of all the relations of production on which they rest, to the abolition of all the social relations that correspond to these relations of production, to the revolutionizing of all the ideas that result from these social relations.[9]

Blanqui and Macfarlane

Macfarlane, in her critique of the Whig conception of history, echoes Blanqui and Marx in declaring that the idea of a constitutional "balance of powers" was "in itself an absurdity, for a state of equilibrium or of rest, not of motion, is what results from the action of 'equally balanced powers,' and at this rate the government of the country would stand still."[10] The Red Republican argument that universal suffrage meant very little in practice without a "social" program, was fuelled by the French experience of the 1848 Revolution. Following the bloody defeat of the workers movement in the "June Days," Louis Napoleon's rapid rise to power in France was based in large part on the "anti-bourgeois" sentiments of the peasantry. Macfarlane argues that, even with universal suffrage, an English squire might be able to lead the politically uneducated laborers on his manor "by the nose." Hence the need for a nationally organized "social propaganda" to help the people raise themselves to the level of self-government. Real democracy could only be "socialist-democracy," or "red republicanism": "Our end is the Organization of Labour and the final establishment of a pure Democracy" to "make it possible for the toiling millions to live in a state more befitting human beings." Revolution would call for "the total destruction of the Past, . . . because existing social forms leave no room for the Evolution of the Democratic Idea"; this revolutionary act would itself be the outcome of "a critique of pure reason."[11]

At the height of Blanqui's influence in the middle of the century, Macfarlane relates the revolts of the helots, bondmen, and serfs through to the 1848 Revolutions as all being part of what Walter Benjamin would later refer to as a "continuum" of history. Benjamin, in his 1939 *Theses on the Philosophy of History*, attacks social democratic Marxism for its inability to see the "the struggling oppressed class itself," rather than abstract "man or men" as the "depository of historical knowledge." Benjamin points out that although in the thought of Marx this class appears as the "avenger" that "completes the task of liberation in

the name of generations of the downtrodden," the social democrats had "within three decades . . . managed to erase the name
of Blanqui" and "thought fit to assign to the working-class the
role of redeemer of future generations, in this way cutting the
sinews of its greatest strength. This training made the working-
class forget both its hatred and spirit of sacrifice, for both are
nourished by the image of enslaved ancestors rather than that of
liberated grandchildren."[12]

After Marx's death in 1883, the Marxists in Germany, despite
the misgivings of Engels, drew their concept of "Practice" from
the organizational innovations of Ferdinand Lassalle, the
founder of the first "mass workers party" in Germany in the
1860s. In the 1860s, Lassalle, much to Marx's disapproval, had
been prepared to negotiate away the most basic principles in
deals with the *Junker* section of the Prussian ruling class, and he
did so without even telling his own supporters. For Blanqui,
such opportunism would have been unthinkable.

While Blanqui remained rooted in the rationalist materialism
of the previous century, Marx's philosophical development—from
1843 to 1883—continually refers back to the ground of his original
critique of Hegel on the relationship between ideas and reality.
Marx's 1844 critique of Hegel demands that philosophy be "capable of grasping the act of world history." What was for Hegel a
2,500-year quest for Freedom as Thought, was for Macfarlane a
2,500-year thread of revolt, enacted as a historical dialectic of
ideas. Concretely, for the organizational needs of the English
Chartists in 1850 this meant:

> If the organisations would fuse into one, with one individual
> centre of Democratic action, a double movement might be car-
> ried on; viz: a crusade for the Charter as a merely political re-
> form, and a veritable revolutionary and social propaganda;
> and that too without distracting the attention of the people by
> the claims of so many Democratic societies.

In Macfarlane's concept of organization, theory had to be more
than just a parade of theories—as in a shopping parade, offering

the "ism" that "suits you best." Macfarlane demands organizational responsibility from theoreticians: that they make themselves useful "without distracting the attention of the people" from the practical issues, and provide, as Marx claims in the *Manifesto*, "critical insight into the conditions, the course, and the general results of real social movement."

Hopes for Chartist Revival

The "Democratic Conference" convened by Harney in August 1850 was initially quite successful in promoting the "Red" program. Not only were the six points of the Peoples Charter upheld, but motions were also passed calling for the redistribution of wealth, nationalization of the land, the ending of legal restrictions on cooperatives, and state support for the old and sick. Passing motions at these meetings did not, however, create real unity. O'Connor and his supporters, having lost control of the N.C.A., regrouped and fought back with Liberal support. One of the Manchester Liberals, Sir Josiah Walmesly, backed an attempt by O'Connor's lieutenant, Thomas Clark, and his supporters on the Manchester Chartist Council to form a breakaway "moderate" Chartism that would remove the "stigma of Redism" from the movement. Some of those involved in Harney's Democratic Conference were wavering and waiting see how Clark's project progressed.[13] Macfarlane comments on the Manchester operation:

> Let these financial and commercial gentlemen, the next time they "do a little" in Machiavelism, to study the adaption of means to ends, else they will bring their goods to a bad market. The infamous Borgia, a pupil of Machiavel . . . did not resemble Sir Joshua Walmesly, for the wily Italian was a man of vigorous intellect, and knew how to chose his instruments.

Clark's operation would soon collapse; Feargus O'Connor, once renowned as the "Lion of the North," was descending into insanity amid the collapse of his Land Scheme. O'Connor's downfall did not, however, herald a revival of Chartist fortunes under the now-unrivalled leadership of the N.C.A. When Ernst Jones was released from prison in June 1850, he launched a new journal, *Notes to the People*, and went on a speaking tour in the North, which drew the largest crowds since 1848. But those who cheered him did not join the N.C.A.

Harney's *Democratic Review* folded at the end of 1850. According to a letter in November 1850 from Marx to Engels, Marx had learned from Jones that Harney was being threatened with prosecution for not paying Stamp Duty on his weekly: "The entire contents of his paper are such as to make it liable to stamp duty. The government is merely waiting for its circulation to increase in order to nab him." Charles Dickens had been having similar trouble and proceedings against Dickens had been "instituted solely as a precedent in respect of Harney. If he is arrested he may, besides the actual sentence, have to serve twenty years through being unable to produce securities."[14] This may have been the reason for Harney's decision to change the name from the *Red Republican*—which was in any case scary to newsagents—to the milder-sounding but still Jacobin-inspired title, *The Friend of the People*. Harney also "softened" the content with a serialization of the George Sand novel *Consuelo* and even brought in some advertising to help cover the costs of publication. Meanwhile, the N.C.A., which since 1842 had never had more than two thousand enrolled in its books, was down to a membership of just five hundred.

Notes

1. Peter Cadogan, "Harney and Engels," *International Review of Social History* X (Amsterdam: 1965), 66–104.

2. *Red Republican,* August 17, 1850.

3. *Democratic Review,* April 1850.

4. *Red Republican,* August 17, 1850.

5. Alisdair MacIntyre, *Whose Justice? Which Rationality?* (London: Duckworth, 1988), 209–39.

6. Walter Kendall, *The Revolutionary Movement in Britain 1900–21* (London: Wiedenfield & Nicolson, 1969).

7. Walter Benjamin, *Charles Baudelaire* (London: Verso, 1976), 16.

8. Bernstein, *Blanqui*, 227.

9. Marx and Engels, *Collected Works Vol. 10*, 127.

10. *Democratic Review,* September 1850.

11. *Democratic Review,* April 1850.

12. Walter Benjamin, *Illuminations* (London: Fontana, 1971), 262–63.

13. Schoyen, *Chartist Challenge*, 208.

14. Marx and Engels, *Collected Works Vol. 38*, 242.

13

"A Rare Bird": Marx's Encounter with Macfarlane

Communist Splits

The Helen Macfarlane story draws to a close on December 31, 1850. The scene is a New Year's Eve banquet organized by the Fraternal Democrats, at the London Literary and Scientific Institute in John Street, near the Tottenham Court Road. Present that evening are various exiled revolutionaries from Hungary, Italy, Poland, France, and Germany (among the latter, Engels and Marx, as well as their erstwhile comrade, Karl Schapper); and members and officers of the Fraternal Democrats including George Holyoake. (Ernst Jones couldn't attend because of illness.) Women known to be present are Jenny Marx, Helen Macfarlane, and Harney's wife, Mary.

Harney makes a speech on the political situation at home and abroad over the last year. He says that there had been "little cause for encouragement," because "nowhere had the people become possessed of institutions which could alone ensure their prosperity in return for their toil." On the other hand, he continues, the year had seen Jones released from prison; the agitation in defense of the draymen who meted out proletarian justice to Field Marshal Haynau had enabled the Society of Fraternal Democrats to extend its "sphere of operations." The year 1850 had also seen Lord Palmerston put under pressure in Parliament because of his "nonintervention" policy regarding Poland and Hungary. Harney denounces Palmerston's failure to protest the killing in Vienna, during the Counterrevolution of 1848, of an Englishman named Baker, who edited a Viennese newspaper called *The Radical*.[1] Finally, Harney calls for international unity until "all Europe resounds to the cry of 'The Republic, Democratic and Social'!"[2]

Engels also addresses the gathering, striking a somewhat less cheering tone than Harney. According to a report the following week in O'Connor's *Northern Star*, he makes "a long and elaborate statement on the causes of failure abroad and consequent reaction," which had been due to "the ignorance of the people and the treachery of their leaders." The revolution, he says, will only come again after "a long struggle, consummated by a new generation of men." Engels's words, however, accurately reported, are clearly intended to ruffle a few feathers among those present and they probably do.

Earlier in the year, Harney, along with Marx and Engels, had been engaged in an attempt to unite the Left of the exiled leaders into a "World League [*Société Universel*] of Revolutionary Socialists" to fight for the "Dictatorship of the Proletariat." In April, the Communist League had assigned August Willich to negotiate the setting up of the "international" with the Fraternal Democrats and the London Blanquists. During that period that Marx had been developing the perspective of "Revolution in Permanence," arguing that although revolutionary workers parties could and would march with the petty bourgeois radicals against the reactionary enemy, they would have to oppose all attempts by the radicals to consolidate their position to the detriment of the workers. The issue came to a head when a new international body was formed, whose politics were quite different to those of the prospective World League of Revolutionary Socialists. The "Central European Democratic Committee, " as it was called, included the moderate socialist, Louis Blanc; the anti-socialists, Ledru-Rollin and Giuseppe Mazzini; and Marx's erstwhile collaborator in Germany, Arnold Ruge. Its somewhat grandiose and vacuous program rejected "the cold and unfeeling travail of the intellect" in favor of the "instinct of the masses" as "the people in motion." To Marx's mind this was tantamount to demanding that the people "have no thought for the morrow and must strike all ideas from the mind" and that "the riddle of the future will be solved by a miracle."[3]

Within the Communist League, Willich and Schapper argued that, despite the defeats suffered by the workers parties in France, the ongoing counterrevolution in Europe would before long force the existing French bourgeois republic to fight against the anciens régimes of Europe. Such a war, they believed, would develop into a War of Liberation that might reopen the floodgates of Revolution. In practice this would mean that in order to find common cause with the petit-bourgeois democrats and nationalists of Europe, the Communists would have to set aside the program of the Dictatorship of the Proletariat. According to Marx, Willich and Schapper "demanded, if not real conspiracies, at least the appearance of conspiracies, and accordingly favoured an alliance with the heroes of the hour."[4]

Marx, who was studying the economic situation in Europe closely, knew that with industry booming, the old order of Europe restabilized, and the bourgeoisie newly confident in its ability to rule, Schapper's perspective was a fantasy. At the September 15 meeting of the central authority of the Communist League, Marx said of Schapper's proposals:

> The revolution is not seen as a product of the *realities* of the situation but as the result of an effort of *will*. Whereas we say to the workers: you have fifteen, twenty, fifty years of civil war to go through in order to alter the situation and to *train* yourselves for the *exercise of power* it is said: we must take power at once, or else we might as well take to our beds. Just as the democrats abused the word "people" so now the word "proletariat" has been used as a mere phrase.[5] [emphasis mine]

Marx pointed out that for communists to make a revolution out of existing forces in the name of the proletariat, they would have to describe the petty-bourgeoisie as proletarian and become *their* representatives. Referring to the 1848 Revolution, he said:

> Louis Blanc is the best example of what happens when you come to power prematurely. In France, moreover, it isn't the

proletariat alone that gains power but the peasants and petty-
bourgeois as well, and it will have to carry out not its but *their*
measures. [emphasis original]

In his reply, Schapper did not try to refute Marx's arguments.
Instead he drew a division between the "party of theory" and
the "party of action" and, somewhat prefiguring the arguments
of the "socialist" dictators of the underdeveloped world of the
twentieth century, said:

> The people who represent the party in principle part company
> with those who organize the proletariat. . . . The question at is-
> sue is whether we ourselves chop off a few heads right at the
> start or whether it is our own heads that will fall. In France the
> workers will come to power and thereby in Germany too. Were
> this not the case I would indeed take to my bed. . . . If we come
> to power we can take such measures as are necessary to ensure
> the role of the proletariat. I am a fanatical supporter of this
> view.[6]

The debate split the League and effectively ended the efforts
to build the World League of Revolutionary Socialists. Schapper,
however, managed to harness Harney to his own plans for revolutionary reorganization, and this led to the formation in November 1850 of a movement, based on Schapper's perspective,
for a "Social Democratic and World Republic" involving the
London Blanquists, the Fraternal Democrats, plus a Polish and a
Hungarian exile group.

Harney's undiminished enthusiasm for organizing banquets
and rallies in the name of international brotherhood drew scorn
from Marx. Referring to Harney as "Mr Hippipharra," Marx
pointed out to Engels that if he was to appear on platforms with
Thomas Clark, the Chartist renegade, Harney would be rightly
outraged; but Harney for his part, did not see any problem with
cooperating with Schapper and "making himself into a
pedestal" for Blanc and all of *"les petits grand hommes"* of the Emigration.[7] As far as Marx was concerned, it was not Louis Blanc,
but Auguste Blanqui who was "true leader of the French proletariat." Harney did not know that Blanqui, incarcerated in Belle-

Ile prison, was less than happy about the actions of his followers in London and would soon break with his London lieutenant, Barthelemy, over the "program peddling" with Ledru-Rollin and Blanc's Central European Democratic Committee. Blanqui, in a statement smuggled out of prison, which was circulated by Marx and Engels, accused his own organization of "hiding its banner, giving ground to the bourgeois republicans and sacrificing the future for the morbid need of uncertain support in the present." Blanqui declared that: "Ideas are the standard of the masses. We must therefore be clear and blunt, and explain everything on pain of being sorely let down. Secrecy is the preliminary of duplicity, and I shall never be party to it."[8]

Macfarlane's Fallout with Harney

We return to the John Street banquet hosted by Harney on New Year's Eve, 1850. What is known of events that night in relation to the fate of Helen Macfarlane comes from a single letter from Marx to Engels some weeks later, telling of the tensions then reaching a breaking point among the London exiles. During this period, the Marxes have been under a lot of stress in their domestic life. They are still mourning the death of their one-year-old son Heinrich six weeks earlier. Jenny, who now is pregnant again, had undertaken a trip to Holland in August on a desperate and fruitless mission to get money from an uncle to help feed their three surviving children and pay the mounting rent arrears for their Dean Street lodgings. While she was away Marx had an affair with their housekeeper, Helene "Lenchen" Demuth. As a result, Lenchen, too is pregnant and Marx is beginning to worry about gossip spreading throughout Soho and reaching his factional enemies at the German Workers Educational Association center in Great Windmill Street. Some weeks later, he will tell Engels that the camp of "Willich, Schapper and Ruge" are "disseminating the most unspeakable infamies about me" and that his sick wife is suffering from "the most disagreeable of domestic quandaries," as well as "exhalations from the pestiferous democratic cloaca" and "stupid tell-tales"[9] The understandable stress Marx must have been under may explain, in part at least, his harsh and slightly "paranoid" tone concerning Mary Harney in a letter to Engels on the subject of the New Year's Eve event. Marx says that while having a great partiality for Louis Blanc, Schapper and the dashing Prussian lieutenant, August Willich, Mary

> hates me as a frivolous person who might become dangerous to her "property to be watched upon" [her husband]. I have definite proof that this woman has got her too long plebeian fingers in the pie here. How much Harney is possessed by this familiar spirit and how sly and narrowly Scots she is you can judge from the following. You will remember how on New Year's Eve, she insulted Helen Macfarlane in the presence of my wife. Later she told my wife with a smiling face that Harney hadn't seen Miss Macfarlane for the whole evening. Later she told him that she had *declined* her acquaintanceship because the cleft dragoon had evoked the dismay and ridicule of the whole company and of my wife in particular. Harney was stupid and cowardly enough not to let her get her own back for the insult, and so break, in the most undignified way, with the only collaborator on his spouting rag who had original ideas—a rare bird, on his paper.[10] [emphasis original]

We are left to wonder about the nature of Mary Harney's insult and whether it could have been enough, along with Harney's "cowardly" reaction to it, to end Macfarlane's fruitful journalistic and political collaboration with him. Mary Harney, a "tall beautiful woman" and "of high spirit," was the daughter of a Chartist radical in Ayrshire.[11] Her animosity toward Macfarlane may have been more political than personal: a case of favoring the "heroes of the hour"—Blanc and perhaps also Willich and Schapper—over Marx and Engels. In any case, the most important revelation in Marx's letter is his statement on how "rare" and "original" he thought Helen Macfarlane was, and how it might suggest that Macfarlane was caught in the middle of the split between Marx/Engels and Harney/Schapper.

Weeks later, Louis Blanc split with the radical democrat Ledru-Rollin; with the third anniversary of the February Revolution approaching, Blanc decided to hold a commemoration in rivalry to one that Rollin was organizing. Blanc succeeded in mobilizing Harney's London Chartists, Schapper's Communists, and Barthelemy's Blanquists for his efforts. Harney, true to form, attempted to strike a neutral pose by speaking at Rollin's event and then rushing off to host Blanc at Highbury Barn, which had a thousand in attendance. When two of Marx's comrades, Conrad Schramm and Wilhelm Pieper, showed up at the Barn, they were denounced as spies by Schapper supporters and beaten up. For Marx, this was the final straw. Although Harney, to his credit, published the victims' own account of the incident in the *Friend of the People* and offered his personal "guarantee" for their "honour" as "introduced to me by Messrs. Marx and Engels, " as far as the latter two were concerned, Harney's organizational efforts were at odds with the *political* principles he had claimed to uphold. Harney, according to Marx, had a "need to have great men to admire, which we have often made fun of in the past. Then he loves theatrical effects. He is certainly a popularity seeker . . . ruled by the phrase and is developing very rich vapidities." Harney, thought Marx, was stuck deeper in the bourgeois democrats' "mud" than he cared to admit.[12] Too deep in fact, for their collaboration to continue. It ended that night and they would not come together again for another twenty-five years.

What became of Helen Macfarlane after the incident on New Year's Eve 1850 is a mystery. As we saw earlier, the census record shows her absence from the Macfarlane household in Burnley on March 30, 1851. Helen may well have moved back to London, at least temporarily, since she was definitely there in December and January. She may have moved because she got married—which might explain why no subsequent writings under the name of "Helen Macfarlane" are listed in sources such as Poole's *Index to Periodical Literature, 1802–1906.* Her absence due to death can be ruled out: firstly, because her demise would surely have been recorded in Harney's presses and probably mentioned in the Marx–Engels–Harney correspondence, and secondly, because some weeks after the census, in April 1851, Harney's *Friend of the People* carried a tiny mention of "H. Morton's fundraising efforts for the Polish and Hungarian refugees in Liverpool threatened with deportation." This refers to the defeated survivors of the Polish Legion who had fought with the Hungarians in a last-ditch stand against the Hapsburg Empire. When their ship arrived in Liverpool, they had refused to board a ship bound for America, despite pressure from the British government who, undesiring of any more resident revolutionaries, had utilized secret service money to pay for their passage.[13] At that point the trail goes cold. Helen Macfarlane *vanishes* from history along with her alias, Howard Morton.

Notes

1. *Northern Star*, January 4, 1851. Marx and Engels, *Collected Works Vol. 10*, 637. The paper *Der Radikale* was connected with the Vienna Workers Association, whose members Marx addressed during the Revolution in September 1848. Marx and Engels, *Collected Works Vol. 38*, 197.

2. Rothstein, *From Chartism to Labourism*, 157

3. Marx and Engels, *Collected Works Vol. 10*, 529–31.

4. Marx, *Herr Vogt*, 28.

5. Marx and Engels, *Collected Works Vol. 10*, 626–28.

6. Marx and Engels, *Collected Works Vol. 10*, 628–29.

7. Schoyen, *Chartist Challenge*, 214.

8. Blanqui's statement is recorded in Marx and Engels, *Collected Works Vol. 10*, 587.

9. Francis Wheen, *Karl Marx* (London: Fourth Estate, 1999), 171–76.

10. Marx to Engels February 23, 1851, in Marx and Engels, *Collected Works Vol. 38*, 291. I have used Schoyens translation, *Chartist Challenge*, 215.

11. G. J. Holyoake, *Sixty Years of an Agitator's Life* (London: 1893). Quoted in Schoyen, *Chartist Challenge*, 104.

12. Marx to Engels, February 23, 1851.

13. Schoyen, *Chartist Challenge*, 212. See also Bernard Porter, *The Refugee Question in Victorian Politics* (Cambridge: Cambridge University Press, 1979).

14

The End of Chartism

The Politics of Trade Unionism

An article by Macfarlane in August 1850, "Middle-class Dodges and Proletarian Gullibility in 1850: A Penny Monument to Sir Robert Peel," comments on the phenomena of "Conservative operatives" in the Manchester Mechanics Institute attempting to recruit subscribers to the forthcoming Great Exhibition in London and a memorial fund for the late anti–Corn Law, Conservative former-prime Minister, Sir Robert Peel:

> If you accept the present system of society without protest, and raise monuments to the man who did all in his power to uphold it—then you must go a step further, you must accept all the results of that system of social arrangements, all the consequences which logically follow from the principles of selfishness and class-legislation at the bottom of that system. Beside the Peel Monument and the Hudson Temple, you must raise altars to famine and pestilence, to physical suffering and moral degradation.[1]

Macfarlane, in the face of the economic developments, appealed to other principles: to reason and history underpinned by revolutionary will. But, as Marx had already recognized, "it is not enough for thought to strive for realization, reality must also strive toward thought." Macfarlane hoped that this dual process was well underway (though she had no illusions about quick results), and Marx and Engels, having articulated this hope in *The Communist Manifesto*, tried to keep it alive as the counterrevolutions were consolidated. But capital had entered a new phase and socialist theory still had to undergo what Hegel called "the labour, suffering, and patience of the negative." By the time Victorian England celebrated "Industry and Empire" at the Great Exhibition in Hyde Park in 1851, the great days of 1848—when, as Walt Whitman put it in a poem printed in the *Red Republican*, "God, 'twas delicious! That brief tight glorious grip, upon the throats of kings"—were beginning to seem quite distant. The British economy was booming and, with the exception of France, every European regime that been toppled in 1848 and 1849 had been restored.

Although the "socialist" program of the "Democratic Conference" in 1850 was formally reaffirmed in April 1851, it did not represent any real unity or impetus "on the ground"; therefore, Harney's "socialist-democratic" party was stillborn. The changes Harney made in his renamed weekly, the *Friend of the People*, failed to increase the circulation, which had never been more than a few thousand. In July 1851, he suspended publication and went on a speaking tour of Scotland and the North to raise support; but he found that his audiences had little zeal for building Chartism back up. When George Holyoake called for unity with Joseph Hume's parliamentary Liberals, the N.C.A backed him, at which point Harney gave up on the organization.

In November 1851, the engineering employers imposed a lockout when Amalgamated Society of Engineers (A.S.E.) demanded an end to overtime and piecework. Since the slump of the early 1840s, the engineering employers' attempts to "deskill" the work process with new technology and piecework had been meeting with stiff resistance. The A.S.E.'s national organizer in 1851, William Newton, had spoken on National Charter Association platforms, but during the strike he rejected an offer by Ernst Jones to address an A.S.E. public meeting, because the union was worried about the strike being seen by the hostile press as "political." The A.S.E. leadership did, however, collaborate with the Christian Socialist "Labour Associations," in a project to establish engineers cooperatives. After the five-month-long strike was defeated, the A.S.E. said that because of "the immense power of wealth and the determination of its possessors," the union could only hope that "a few years will see the land studded with workshops belonging to the workers," in which "the artisan may successfully assert his claim to be treated as a man with thoughts and feelings instead of a machine."[2] From this defeat, Jones drew the lesson that the trade unionists showed little grasp of the power of capital:

> Strikes and cooperations they can meet, because you have not the money for it—they have; but political combinations they cannot resist, because they have not the numbers, and you have.[3]

In 1852 Harney took over the *Northern Star*, whose circulation had dropped to just twelve hundred and merged it with the newly revived *Friend of the People* as a new title, the *Star of Freedom*. But by this time Jones was publishing the *People's Paper* and complained that Harney "must well know two such papers cannot at present exist together." But Jones knew himself that there were serious political differences between the two, especially over the role of trade unions, who he thought were becoming the "aristocracy of labour," and cooperators, whose schemes he said amounted to "profiteering." Harney countered that, with the political campaign for the Charter at a low ebb, Jones would be wise not to "make enemies of men whom it was desirable to have as friends and fellow labourers in the cause of social justice." The cooperative movement, Harney hoped, would give an impetus to "Social Regeneration." The "next great political movement" would be *"democratique* and *sociale"*; the co-ops and unions would "advance the discussion of social principles, and thereby prepare the way for those Social Revolutionists who seek through Universal Suffrage, the Abolition of Classes and the Sovereignty of Labour." If Parliament failed to ease the legal obstructions facing the cooperatives, unions and friendly societies then, come the next economic crisis, would be politicized again. In the

1852 elections, Harney's paper campaigned for A.S.E. leader Newton as a Labour and Cooperative candidate for London Tower Hamlets. Newton, however, did badly at the poll, as did Harney at Bradford—although Jones did well at Halifax, winning the show of hands. In September 1852, Newton called for a new "National Party" based on the single issue of Male Suffrage. Harney decided to support it as the best hope of renewal, but Jones attacked it as yet another "middle-class dodge." As it turned out, Newton had second thoughts about chances of success and failed to attend a launch-meeting for the party. At that point Harney gave up on party-building and withdrew from the movement.[4]

Marx's report on the National Party in the *New York Daily Tribune* (November 25, 1852) bemoans the "miserable compromises and backslidings" and draws comparison with the failures of the "democrats" of Ancient Rome during the Cataline Rebellion:

> Cataline is at the gates of the city, a decisive struggle is drawing near, the opposition knows its unpopularity, its incapacity for resistance, and all attempts at the formation of new centres of defence agree in one point only, in a "going backwards policy." The "National Party" retreats from the Charter to General suffrage [the Little Charter], Joe Hume from General Suffrage to the ballot, a third from the ballot to the equalisation of electoral districts, and so forth, until at last we arrive at [Liberal leader] Johnny Russell, who has nothing to give out for a battle cry but the mere name of democracy.[5]

Did Marx Understand Chartism?

Peter Cadogan accuses Marx and Engels of "siding" with Jones against Harney in the trade union dispute and judges them guilty of "sectarianism." Cadogan, however, does not sufficiently take into account the European dimension of the Communist–Chartist relationship. As indicated in the previous chapter, there were real principles at stake in Marx's arguments with those European revolutionaries-in-exile, who, in Marx's opinion were using Harney as a "pedestal." The accusation of "taking sides" does not quite square with Marx's complaint to Engels: that the Harney–Jones dispute was "on the level of German emigrants' polemics." Of Marx's agreement to be elected as an honorary delegate to Jones's "Labour Parliament" in 1854 along with Louis Blanc, Cadogan claims: "There is nothing to suggest that he [Marx] did not attach some significance to it. From this it is quite apparent he was wholly out of touch with the situation,"—that is, that "Chartism was near its last gasp . . . while the fact of his giving Jones support as in 1851–52 only made matters worse."[6]

In 1853, Jones in fact did a turnaround from his previous position on trade unions, when he sensed a new mood of labor militancy. Jones told Marx that since the new "labour movement rose on the ruins of the political one," the resistance of Parliament to pro-labor reforms "had thrown a more revolutionary tendency in the labour-mind." The opportunity was "thus afforded for rallying the masses around the standard of real Social Reform" and for "uniting the scattered ranks of Chartism on the sound principles of social revolution." Marx certainly liked the idea of a Labour Parliament—which, one can imagine, may have struck a chord in the popular imagination—and wished the venture well. But turning to Marx's letter to the Labour Parliament (he didn't attend in person), we find nothing in it relating to the Jones–Harney dispute—which had in any case ended a year previously with Harney's departure following the dashing of his hopes for Chartist–Trade Union–Cooperative unity. What Marx does pose is the question of economic power: English workers, having fulfilled the first condition of emancipation by creating the "productive powers of modern industry," now had to realize "its other condition" to

> free those wealth-producing shackles of monopoly, and subject them to the joint control of the producers, who, till now, allowed the very products of their hands to turn against them and be transformed into as many instruments of their own subjugation.[7]

Jones took an "ultra-vanguardist" position: that although it would "take millions to wage a social war—a few thousands can carry a political movement through its widest ramifications." Marx told Engels that Jones tended toward "a tactless fumbling after pretexts for agitation and restless desire to move faster than the times."

The Economics of Defeat

The June 1848 Counterrevolution in France established, in Macfarlane's words, "a system of bourgeois terrorism—of odious sanguinary despotism—to which it would be difficult to find a match in the history of any civilized nation." But in the years following Louis Napoleon's coup d'état of December 1851, it became apparent to Marx that the stability of the regime depended as much on its economic innovations as on political repression. Bonapartism, having presented itself as the "third force" that had saved France from the "despotism" of the bourgeois National Assembly as well as the "anarchy" of the "Reds," had one great innovative weapon: *Credit*. Marx analyzed the Credit Mobilier investment bank as "one of the most curious phenomena of our epoch." This "creature" of Louis Napoleon's "imperial socialism" had acquired a large part of shares in French industry and then issued ten times that volume as "joint shares" of its own making. Bonaparte's bankers, in attempting to fuel a new "take-off" for French Imperialism by means of credit and speculation, had taken onboard the economic ideology of Saint-Simon and "utopian socialism," and had emphasized the power of "association" over "greed" and "competition." Proudhon had argued that the capital–labour relationship could find a "right" level of "equal" exchange values within simple circulation. In 1849, Proudhon attempted to harness the "force of association" through free credit by launching his *Bank de Peuple*, a venture that collapsed almost immediately. Serge Bologna highlights these popular illusions regarding the power of financial innovation to secure the "full fruits of labour" and points out that "the historical significance of money speculation resides precisely in the fact that it avoids a direct relationship with the working-class." Speculation is a flight of capital from its source, the depreciation of labor that comes about through increased mechanization. So was it any accident, Bologna asks, that Marx aired his analysis of the "Revolution from Above" before an audience of English Chartists, who were being pulled toward the Liberal camp by would-be "financial reformers"?[8]

The class-compromise resulting from the engineers' defeat in 1851 did not bring cooperatives, but new subordinate relationships of labor to capital at the point of production. The new stage of capitalist production, in which King Cotton was being eclipsed in the Age of Steel, required an expanded sector dedicated to the production of means of production. Relations of authority in the workplace changed decisively as an increasingly large number of male skilled workers in engineering and cotton were assigned to the roles of pacemakers and taskmasters over workers on the new machines. With the railway boom and the global expansion of trade and colonialism, British foundries and engineering works were becoming the sources of super-profits. Employers were beginning to see unions in a less hostile light, because unions were themselves changing. Schoyen points out that, "the elite workers who were benefiting from the increase in industrialization—e.g., the skilled mechanics—already had an interest in preserving the economic system."[9] The majority of proletarians were left outside of the trade unions: women workers in clothing and textiles, who numbered over a million by 1851; children, who at that time still comprised nearly 10 percent of the total industrial workforce; and the mass of unskilled manual workers in the new industries such as railways and steel.[10]

Parliament was also changing its attitude to unions and the cooperatives, partly because of vigorous lobbying efforts by the Christian Socialists and their parliamentary allies. As early as 1852, the government began to lift the main legal obstacles on cooperatives and friendly societies; the credit boom of 1852 through 1857 further integrated them into the system. By this time, Parliament had already brought in the Ten Hours Act, the Factory Acts, public health legislation, the Peelite banking reforms, and the repeal of the Corn Laws. The Cobden–Bright radicals of the Manchester School had, for their part, tried the trick of stoking the class struggle to frighten the aristocracy once too often; their electoral deals with Labour were spurned by the middle-class voters, who elected a Liberal government led by Lord Palmerston in 1855. The Manchester radicals had portrayed the electoral struggle as between the "industrious classes" and the landowner–finance aristocracy allied with big industrial and mercantile capital; but, as Bologna points out, it was the latter stratum that represented the forces of *social* capital under a banking system, now reformed so as to oil the wheels of speculation and imperial expansion. As British supremacy in manufacturing was now being challenged by new industrial powers in the world, the ideology of Free Trade was giving way to Anglo-Saxon nationalism, imperialism, and protectionism. Marx compared Palmerston with Louis Napoleon: "One saved France from a social crisis; the other wants to save England from a continental crisis." In 1857, the 1850s credit and trade boom burst, just as Marx had predicted it would. Marx hoped that the breakup of the old alliance of bourgeois and working-class radicals would lead to an independent working-class party. Class struggle, now abandoned by the "productivist" bourgeoisie as a lever for its own use, could from now on only benefit the working class. But if Marx's immediate hopes rested on Ernst Jones's ability to provide the lead now that Harney and Macfarlane were no longer active, he was soon disappointed. After the failure of the 1854 "Labour Parliament" initiative, Jones kept Chartist journalism going until the late 1850s, by which time he had decided that working with the Liberals was the best way to gain the suffrage. After twenty years, Chartism was dead.

Notes

1. *Red Republican*, August 3, 1850.
2. *Labour's Formative Years 1849–79*, ed. J. J. Jeffreys (London: Lawrence and Wishart, 1948), 58–59.
3. *Notes*, 860–62.
4. Schoyen, *Chartist Challenge*, 226–28.

5. Marx and Engels, *Collected Works Vol. 11*, 373.

6. Peter Cadogan, "The Origins of Sectarianism," *Labour Review*, December 1958.

7. Marx and Engels, *Collected Works Vol. 13*, 61.

8. Serge Bologna, "Marx on Money," *Common Sense: Journal of Edinburgh Conference of Socialist Economists*, nos. 13 and 14, 1993–1994.

9. Shoyen, *Chartist Challenge*, 232–33.

10. Foster, *Class Struggle and the Industrial Revolution*, 250.

15

The Legacy of Hegelian Marxism

Techow "imagines" that I have composed a "proletarian catechism." . . . [He] further "imagines" that I have "tailored" a "system," while, on the contrary, even in the "[Communist] Manifesto," which was intended directly for workers, I rejected all systems, and in their place put "the critical insight into the conditions, the course, and the general results of real social movement." Such an insight, however, can neither be conjured up nor "tailored" to order.

—Karl Marx, *Herr Vogt*, 1860

Alas! We know that the battle between the old and new epochs—between falsehood and truth, selfishness and love, despotism and freedom—will be long, bloody and terrible. Through revolutions which have already begun, through fearful social convulsions, through wars and calamities, will the children of light triumph—after long years, it may be—over the powers of darkness. The Greek myth sets forth, that Hercules conquered the kingdom of heaven by his valour, only after a long series of labours and sufferings, and at the last—a painful death—was he admitted among the Gods, and united to Hebe, the personification of immortal youth and joy. This is as true now as it was in the days of Homer—or earlier—when all men devoutly believed it. We must work, then, before we can enter our heaven. [emphasis original]

—Helen Macfarlane, *Democracy*, 1850

In the *Confidence Man*, written in 1857, Herman Melville remarks on the rarity of original characters both in fiction and in life: "Characters, merely singular, imply but singular forms," while original characters "imply original instincts." Melville says that "a due conception" of the original personage in fiction would "make him almost as much of a prodigy there, as in real history is a law-giver, a revolutionizing philosopher, or the founder of a new religion." Dunayevskaya quotes Melville's observations to support her own assessment of Rosa Luxemburg as one such original in "real history," one who—rather like Macfarlane's mythical Antigone—"combines yesterday, today, and tomorrow in such a manner that the new age suddenly experiences a 'shock of recognition,' whether that relates to a new lifestyle or the great need for a revolution here and now."[1]

Macfarlane's known work spanned only a short period in mid-nineteenth-century England; she never got to lead mass movements or write major theoretical works as did Luxemburg before she was murdered by the *Freikorps* in 1918 Berlin. Nevertheless, just as the study of how original ideas spread their influence is important, so is the question of why, how, where, when, and in whom such ideas arise and take hold in the first place. Helen Macfarlane was indeed a rare "original character"; her expression of "Hegelian-Marxism"—though undeveloped and cut short—seems to me still relevant and still resonant. In Hegel's philosophy, the "cunning of reason" works through the development of human consciousness toward a full concept of Freedom. In Macfarlane's interpretation, the "democratic idea" is the process by which twenty-five thousand years of struggle in thought and in life finally results in the "practical realization" of a "golden age," "without poor, without classes . . . not only of free men but of free *women*" (emphasis original).

The question that faced Macfarlane, Harney, Marx, and Engels in 1850—of how an aspiring historical movement, having achieved a certain "grasp of world history," could then use that insight to help make history—took on a new urgency for post-Marx Marxists in the twentieth century, when that "insight" itself became an objective factor *in* history with the Russian and German Revolutions of 1917 and 1918, following the collapse of the old Empires of Europe, which had survived the storms of 1848. The Revolutions did indeed face "fearful social convulsions, through wars and calamities." Furthermore, the "forms" that the movement took in the twentieth century (Social Democracy, Stalinism, etc.) were based on economic determinism rather than a concept of Freedom; if, as Joachim Ritter puts it, the "historical principle of society's emancipatory constitution," as expressed in Hegel's *Philosophy of Right*, was the "nature principle of society" as taken over from political economy, then it would seem that the twentieth century saw that principle transformed into the political *practice* of state power, including totalitarian Communism. With the implosion of Communism in the late 1980s, Francis Fukuyama, in a superficially Hegelian fashion, revived Alexander Kojeve's thesis that Bolshevism, and Leftism generally, had been mere continuations of the Jacobinism of the French Revolution. Fukuyama concluded that this time we really had reached the "End of History." Revolution had been a painful, but historically "necessary" determination of what Hegel called the "slaughterbench" of history, in its overcoming of internal and external obstacles to a rational order of civil society. From this point of view, the Hegelian idea of Freedom, which Helen Macfarlane thought could only be realized by socialism, actually came to fruition when the Berlin Wall came down and the "free market" invaded the decrepit state-capitalist economies of the Eastern Bloc. This collapse of "Communism"—in reality it was a system in which the value–form of alienated labor was just as deeply embedded as in the West—strengthened the move toward globalization. The globalization process was, however, envisaged in *The Communist Manifesto* of 1848 as the Faustian spirit that "negates all": "The Bourgeoisie can exist only under the condition of continuously revolutionising machinery, or the instruments of Production. That is, perpetually changing the system of production, which again amounts to changing the whole system of social arrangements." The changes in "arrangements" take in the whole world: "The need of an ever-increasing market for their produce, drives the Bourgeoisie over the whole globe . . . Instead of the old local and national feeling of self-sufficingness and isolation, we find a universal intercourse, an interdependence, amongst nations. The same fact obtains in the intellectual world. The intellectual productions of individual nations tend to become common property." Although the "commercial crises" undermine the system—"destroying masses of productive power"—at the same time they help to renovate it and spread it, by opening up new markets and using up the old ones more thoroughly, even though "they prepare the way for still more universal and dangerous crises, and reduce the means of withstanding them."

This insight—that it was precisely the universalization of capital that would would lead to its overthrow—was deepened in Marx's *Capital* in 1867: the commodity form would bring forth its negation-from-below by revolutionary subjects who, in their "quest for universality" would uproot the capital-producing system and replace it with a sustainable and free society fit for humans.

Whether of not this perspective was right remains to be seen. But inasmuch as the dialectic of Capital and Labour will determine the outcome of the process, we could do worse than heed Hegel's warning that the Idea cannot be simply be "denied objective validity because it lacks that which constitutes appearance, or the untrue being of the objective world."[2]

Notes

1. Raya Dunayevsakya, *Rosa Luxemburg, Womens Liberation, and Marx's Philosophy of Revolution* (Atlantic Highlands, N.J.: Humanities Press, 1982), 83–86.
2. Hegel, *Science of Logic*, 756.

Appendix A

The Published Writings of Helen Macfarlane

Democratic Review

As Helen Macfarlane

Issues April, May, and June 1850, "Democracy: Remarks on the Times Apropos of Certain Passages in No. 1 of Thomas Carlyle's 'Latter-Day' Pamphlet."

As Howard Morton

July 1850, "Intrigues of the Middle-Class Reformers."
September 1850, "A Birds Eye View of the Glorious British Constitution."

Red Republican

As Howard Morton

June 22, 1850, "Chartism in 1850."
July 13, 1850, "The Red Flag in 1850."
July 20, 1850, "Fine Words (Household or Otherwise) Butter No Parsnips."

August 3, 1850, "Middle-Class Dodges and Proletarian Gullibility in 1850: A Penny Monument to Sir Robert Peel."

August 17, 1850, "Democratic Organisation."

September 14, 1850, "Proceedings of the Peace-at-Any-Price Middle-class Humbugs."

September 21, 1850, "The Morning Post and the Woman Flogger."

October 12, 1850, "The Democratic and Social Republic."

November 2 and 9, 1850, "Labour versus Capital: Two Chapters on Humbug."

November 9, 16, 23, and 30, Translation of the "Manifesto of the Communist Party of Germany in four parts."

Friend of the People

As Howard Morton

December 21 and 26, 1850 "Signs of the Times: Red Stockings versus Lawn-Sleeves" [in two parts].

Appendix B

The Communist Manifesto: Helen Macfarlane's 1850 Translation

The Manifesto of the German Communist Party

[George Julian Harney's introduction: *Red Republican*, November 9, 1850]

The following Manifesto, which has since been adopted by all fractions of German Communists, was drawn up in the German language, in January 1848, by Citizens Charles Marx and Frederic Engels. It was immediately printed in London, in the German language, and published a few days before the outbreak of the Revolution of February. The turmoil consequent upon that great event made it impossible to carry out, at that time, the intention of translating it into all the languages of civilized Europe. There exist two different French versions of it in manuscript, but under the present oppressive laws of France, the publication of either of them has been found impracticable. The English reader will be enabled, by the following excellent translation of this important document, to judge of the plans and principles of the most advanced party of the German Revolutionists. It must not be forgotten, that the whole of this Manifesto was written and printed before the Revolution of February.

A frightful hobgoblin stalks throughout Europe. We are haunted by a ghost, the ghost of Communism. All the Powers of the Past have joined in a holy crusade to lay this ghost to rest—the Pope and the Czar, Metternich and Guizot, French Radicals and German police agents.

Where is the opposition which has not been accused of Communism by its enemies in Power? And where the opposition that has not hurled this blighting accusation at the heads of the more advanced oppositionists, as well as at those of its official enemies?

Two things appear on considering these facts.

1. The ruling Powers of Europe acknowledge Communism to be also a Power.
2. It is time for the Communists to lay before the world an account of their aims and tendencies and to oppose these silly fables about "the bugbear of Communism" by a manifesto of the Communist Party.[1]

Chapter 1[2]

Freemen and Slaves, Patricians and Plebeians, Nobles and Serfs, Members of Guilds and Journeymen,—in a word, the oppressors and the oppressed, have always stood in direct opposition to each other. The battle between them has sometimes been open, sometimes concealed, but always continuous. A never-ceasing battle, which has invariably ended, either in a revolutionary alteration of the social system, or in the common destruction of the hostile classes.

In the earlier historical epochs we find almost everywhere a minute division of Society into classes or ranks, a variety of grades in social position. In ancient Rome we find Patricians, Knights, Plebeians, Slaves, in Mediaeval Europe, Feudal Lords, Vassals, Burghers, Journeymen, Serfs; and in each of these classes there were again grades and distinctions.

Modern Bourgeois Society, proceeded from the ruins of the feudal system, but the Bourgeois regime has not abolished the antagonism of classes. New classes, new conditions of oppression, new forms and modes of carrying on the struggle, have been substituted for the old ones.

The characteristic of our Epoch, the Era of the Middle-class, or Bourgeoisie, is that struggle between the various Social Classes, has been reduced to its simplest form. Society incessantly tends to be divided into two great camps, into two great hostile armies, the Bourgeoisie and the Proletariat.

The burgesses of the early Communes sprang from the Serfs of the Middle Ages. From the Municipal class were developed the primitive elements of the modern Bourgeoisie.

The discovery of the New World, the circumnavigation of Africa, gave the Middle class—then coming into being—new fields of action. The colonization of America, the opening up of the East Indian and Chinese markets, the Colonial Trade. The increase of commodities generally and of the means of exchange, gave an impetus, hitherto unknown, to Commerce, Shipping and the revolutionary element in the old decaying feudal form of society.

The old feudal way of managing the industrial interest by means of guilds and monopolies was not found sufficient for the increased demand caused by the opening up of these new markets. It was replaced by the manufacturing system. Guilds vanished before the industrial Middle-class, and the division of labour between the different corporations was succeeded by the division of labour between the workmen of one and the same great workshop.

But the demand always increased, new markets came into play. The manufacturing system, in its turn, was found to be inadequate. At this point industrial Production was revolutionised by machinery and steam. The modern industrial system was developed in all its gigantic proportions; instead of the industrial Middle-class we find industrial millionaires, chiefs of whole industrial armies, the modern Bourgeois, or Middle-class Capitalists.

The discovery of America was the first step towards the formation of a colossal market, embracing the whole world; whereby an immense development of the Bourgeoisie, the increase of their

Capital, the superseding of all classes handed down to modern times from the Middle Ages, kept pace with the development of Production, Trade, and Steam communication.

We find, therefore, that the modern Bourgeoisie are themselves the result of a long process of development, of a series of revolutions in the modes of Production and Exchange. Each of the degrees of industrial revolution, passed through by the modern Middle-class, was accompanied by a corresponding degree of political development. This class was oppressed under the feudal regime, it then assumed the form of armed and self-regulating associations in the mediaeval Municipalities; in one country we find it existing as a commercial republic, or free town; in another, as the third taxable Estate of the Monarchy; then during the prevalence of the manufacturing system (before the introduction of steam power) the Middle-class was a counterpoise to the Nobility in absolute Monarchies, and the groundwork of the powerful monarchical States generally. Finally, since the establishment of the modern industrial system, with its world-wide market, this class has gained the exclusive possession of political power in modern representative States. Modern Governments are merely Committees for managing the common affairs of the whole Bourgeoisie.

This Bourgeoisie has occupied an extremely revolutionary position in History.

As soon as the Bourgeois got the upper hand, they destroyed all feudal, patriarchal, idyllic relationships between men. They relentlessly tore asunder the many-sided links of that feudal chain which bound men to their "natural superiors," and they left no bond of union between man and man, save that of bare self-interest, of cash payments. They changed personal dignity into market value, and substituted the single unprincipled freedom of trade for the numerous, hardly earned, chartered liberties of the Middle Ages. Chivalrous enthusiasm, the emotions of piety, vanished before the icy breath of their selfish calculations. In a word, the Bourgeoisie substituted shameless, direct, open spoliation, for the previous system of spoliation concealed under religious and political illusions.

They stripped off that halo of sanctity which had surrounded the various modes of human activity, and had made them ven-

erable, and venerated. They changed the physician, the jurispru-
dent, the priest, the poet, the philosopher, into their hired ser-
vants.

They tore the touching veil of sentiment from domestic ties,
and reduced family-relations to a mere question of hard cash.

The Middle-classes have shown how the brutal physical
force of the Middle Ages, so much admired by Reactionists,
found its befitting complement in the laziest ruffianism. They
have also shown what human activity is capable of accomplish-
ing. They have done quite other kinds of marvellous work than
Egyptian pyramids, Roman aqueducts, or Gothic Cathedrals;
and their expeditions have far surpassed all former Crusades,
and Migrations of nations.

The Bourgeoisie can exist only under the condition of continuously revolutionising machinery, or the instruments of Production. That is, perpetually changing the system of production,
which again amounts to changing the whole system of social
arrangements. Persistence in the old modes of Production was,
on the contrary, the first condition of existence for all the preceding industrial Classes. A continual change in the modes of
Production, a never ceasing state of agitation and social insecurity, distinguish the Bourgeois-Epoch from all preceding ones.
The ancient ties between men, their opinions and beliefs—hoar
with antiquity—are fast disappearing, and the new ones become
worn out ere they can become firmly rooted. Every thing fixed
and stable vanishes, everything holy and venerable is desecrated, and men are forced to look at their mutual relations, at
the problem of Life, in the soberest, the most matter of fact way.

The need of an ever-increasing market for their produce,
drives the Bourgeoisie over the whole globe—they are forced to
make settlements, to form connections, to set up means of communication everywhere.

Through their command of a universal market, they have
given a cosmopolitan tendency to the production and consump-
tion of all countries. To the great regret of the Reactionists, the
Bourgeoisie have deprived the modern Industrial System of its national foundation. The old national manufactures have been, or are
being, destroyed. They are superseded by new modes of industry,

whose introduction is becoming a vital question for all civilized nations, whose raw materials are not indigenous, but are brought from the remotest countries, and whose products are not merely consumed in the home market, but throughout the whole world. Instead of the old national wants, supplied by indigenous products, we everywhere find new wants, which can be supplied only by the productions of the remotest lands and climes. Instead of the old local and national feeling of self-sufficingness and isolation, we find a universal intercourse, an inter-dependence, amongst nations. The same fact obtains in the intellectual world. The intellectual productions of individual nations tend to become common property. National one-sidedness and mental limitation are fast becoming impossible, and a universal literature is being formed from the numerous national and local literatures.

Through the incessant improvements in machinery and the means of locomotion, the Bourgeoisie draw the most barbarous savages into the magic circle of civilization. Cheap goods are their artillery for battering down Chinese walls, and their means of overcoming the obstinate hatred entertained towards strangers by semi-civilized nations. The Bourgeoisie, by their competition, compel, under penalty of inevitable ruin, the universal adoption of their system of production; they force all nations to accept what is called civilization—to become Bourgeois—and thus the middle class fashions the world anew after its own image.

The Bourgeoisie has subjected the *country* to the ascendancy of the *town*; it has created enormous cities, and, by causing an immense increase of population in the manufacturing, as compared with the agricultural districts, has saved a great part of every people from the idiotism of country life. Not only have the Bourgeoisie made the country subordinate to the town, they have made barbarous and half-civilized tribes dependent on civilized nations, the agricultural on the manufacturing nations, the East on the West.

The division of property, of the means of production, and of population, vanish under the Bourgeois regime. It agglomerates population, it centralises the means of production, and concentrates property in the hands of a few individuals. Political centralization is the necessary consequence of this. Independent provinces, with different interests, each of them surrounded by a separate line of customs and under separate local governments, are brought together as one nation, under the same government, laws, line of customs, tariff, the same national class-interest.

The Bourgeois regime has only prevailed for about a century, but during that time it has called into being more gigantic powers of production than all preceding generations put together. The subjection of the elements of nature, the development of machinery, the application of chemistry to agriculture and manufactures, railways, electric telegraphs, steam ships, the clearing and cultivation of whole continents, canalizing of thousands of rivers; large populations, whole industrial armies, springing up, as if by magic! What preceding generation ever dreamed of these productive powers slumbering within society?

We have seen that these means of production and traffic which served as the foundation of middle-class development, originated in feudal times. At a certain point in the evolution of these means, the arrangements under which feudal society produced and exchanged the feudal organization of agriculture and industrial production,—in a word, the feudal conditions of property—no longer corresponded to the increased productive power. These conditions now became a hindrance to it—they were turned into fetters which had to be broken, and they were broken.

They were superseded by unlimited competition, with a suitable social and political constitution, with the economical and political supremacy of the middle class.

At the present moment a similar movement is going on before our eyes. Modern middle-class society, which has revolutionised the conditions of property, and called forth such colossal means of production and traffic, resembles the wizard who evoked the powers of darkness, but could neither master them, nor yet get rid of them when they had come at his bidding. The history of manufactures and commerce has been for many years the history of the revolts of modern productive power against the modern industrial system—against the modern conditions of property—which are vital conditions, not only of the supremacy of the middle-class, but of its very existence. It suffices to mention the commercial crises which, in each of their periodical occurrences, more and more endanger the existence of middle-class society. In such a crisis, not only is a quantity of industrial products destroyed, but a large portion of the productive power itself. A social epidemic breaks out, the epidemic of over-production, which would have appeared a contradiction in terms to all previous generations. Society finds itself suddenly thrown back into momentary barbarism; a famine, a devastating war, seems to have deprived it of the means of subsistence; manufactures and commerce appear annihilated,—and why? Because society possesses too much civilisation, too many of the necessaries of life, too much industry, too much commerce. The productive power possessed by society no longer serves as the instrument of middle-class civilization, of the middle-class conditions of property; on the contrary, this power has become too mighty for this system, it is forcibly confined by these conditions; and whenever it surpasses these artificial limitations, it deranges the system of Bourgeois society, it endangers the existence of Bourgeois property. The social system of the middle-class has become too small to contain the riches it has called into being. How does the middle-class try to withstand these commercial crises? On the one hand, by destroying masses of productive power; on the other, by opening up new markets, and using up the old ones more thoroughly. That is, they prepare the way for still more universal and dangerous crises, and reduce the means of withstanding them.

The weapons with which the middle-class overcame feudalism are now turned against the middle-class itself.

And the Bourgeoisie have not only prepared the weapons for their own destruction, they have also called into existence the men that are destined to wield these weapons, namely, the modern working men, the Proletarians.

The development of the Proletariat has kept pace with the development of the middle-class—that is, with the development of capital; for the modern working men can live only as long as they find work, and they find it only as long as their labour increases capital. These workers, who must sell themselves by piecemeal to the highest bidder, are a commodity like other articles of commerce, and, therefore, are equally subject to all the variations of the market, and the effects of competition.

Through the division of labour and the extension of machinery, work has lost its individual character, and therefore its interest for the operative. He has become merely an accessory to, or a part of the machine, and all that is required of him is a fatiguing, monotonous, and merely mechanical operation. The expense the wages-slave causes the capitalist is, therefore, equal to the cost of his keep and of the propagation of his race. The price of labour, like that of any other commodity, is equal to the cost of its production. Therefore wages decrease in proportion as the work to be performed becomes mechanical, monotonous, fatiguing, and repulsive. Further, in proportion as the application of machinery and the division of labour increase, the amount of work increases also, whether it be through an increase in the hours of work, or in the quantity of it demanded in a given time, or through an increased rate of velocity of the machinery employed.

The modern industrial system has changed the little shop of the primitive patriarchal master into the large factory of the Bourgeois–capitalist. Masses of operatives are brought together in one establishment, and organized like a regiment of soldiers; they are placed under the superintendence of a complete hierarchy of officers and sub-officers. They are not only the slaves of the whole middle-class (as a body), of the Bourgeois political regime,—they are the daily and hourly slaves of the machinery, of the foreman, of each individual manufacturing Bourgeois. This despotism is the more hateful, contemptible, and aggravating, because gain is openly proclaimed to be its only object and aim.

In proportion as labour requires less physical force and less dexterity—that is, in proportion to the development of the modern industrial system—is the substitution of the labour of women and children for that of men. The distinctions of sex and age have no social meaning for the Proletarian class. Proletarians are merely so many instruments which cost more or less, according to their sex and age.

When the using-up of the operative has been so far accomplished by the mill-owner that the former has got his wages, the rest of the Bourgeoisie, householders, shopkeepers, pawnbrokers, &c., fall upon him like so many harpies.

The petty Bourgeoisie, the inferior ranks of the middle-class, the small manufacturers, merchants, tradesmen, and farmers, tend to become Proletarians, partly because their small capital succumbs to the competition of the millionaire, and partly because the modes of production [are] perpetually changing, their peculiar skill loses its value. Thus the Proletariat is recruited from various sections of the population.

This Proletarian class passes through many phases of development, but its struggle with the middle-class dates from its birth. At first the struggle is carried on by individual workmen, then by those belonging to a single establishment, then by those of an entire trade in the same locality, against the individuals of the middle-class who directly use them up. They attack not only the middle-class system of production, but even the instruments of production; they destroy machinery and the foreign commodities which compete with their products; they burn down factories, and try to re-attain the position occupied by the producers of the middle ages.

At this moment of development, the Proletariat forms a disorganized mass, scattered throughout the country, and divided by competition. A more compact union is not the effect of their own development, but is the consequence of a middle-class union; for the Bourgeoisie requires, and for the moment are still enabled, to set the whole Proletariat in motion, for the furtherance of their own political ends; developed in this degree, therefore, the Proletarians do not fight their own enemies, but the enemies of their enemies, the remains of absolute monarchy, the land-owners, the non-manufacturing part of the Bourgeoisie and the petty shopocracy. The whole historical movement is thus, as yet, concentrated in the hands of the Bourgeoisie, every victory is won for them.

But the increase of the Proletariat keeps pace with the evolution of production; the working-class is brought together in masses, and learns its own strength. The interests and position of different trades become similar, because machinery tends to reduce wages to the same level, and to make less and less difference between the various kinds of labour. The increasing competition amongst the middle-class, and the commercial crises consequent thereupon, make wages always more variable, while the incessant improvements in machinery make the position of the Proletarians more and more uncertain, and the collisions between the individual workmen and the individual masters, assume more and more the character of collisions between two classes. The workmen commence to form trades-unions against the masters; they turn out, to prevent threatened reductions in their wages. They form associations to help each other in, and to provision themselves for these occasional revolts. Here and there the struggle takes the form of riots.

From time to time the Proletarians are, for a moment, victorious, yet the result of their struggle is not an immediate advantage, but the ever increasing union amongst their class. This union is favoured by the facility of communication under the modern industrial system, whereby the Proletarians belonging to the remotest localities are placed in connection with each other. But connection is all that is wanting to change innumerable local struggles, having all the same character, into one national struggle—into a battle of classes. Every battle between different classes is a political battle, and the union, which it took the burghers of the middle ages centuries to bring about, by means of their few and awkward roads, can be accomplished in a few years by the modern Proletarians, by means of railways and steamships.

This organisation of the Proletarians into a class, and therewith into a political party, is incessantly destroyed by the competitive principle. Yet it always reappears, and each time it is stronger and more extensive. It compels the legal acknowledgment of detached Proletarian rights, by profiting of the divisions in the *bourgeois* camp. For example, the Ten Hours' Bill in England.

The struggles of the ruling classes amongst themselves are favourable to the development of the Proletariat. The middle-class has always been in a state of perpetual warfare—first, against the aristocracy; and then against that part of itself whose interests are opposed to the further evolution of the industrial system; and, thirdly, against the bourgeoisie of other countries. During all of these battles, the middle-class has ever been obliged to appeal for help to the Proletarians, and so to draw the latter into the political movement. This class, therefore, has armed the Proletarians against itself, by letting them share in its own means of cultivation.

Further, as we have already seen, the evolution of the industrial system has thrown a large portion of the ruling class into the ranks of the Proletarians, or at least rendered the means of subsistence very precarious for this portion. A new element of progress for the Proletariat.

Finally, as the settlement of the class-struggle draws near, the process of dissolution goes on so rapidly within the ruling-class—within the worn-out body politic—that a small fraction of this class separates from it, and joins the revolutionary class, in whose hands lies the future. In the earlier revolutions a part of the *noblesse* joined the *bourgeoisie,* in the present one, a part of the *bourgeoisie* is joining the Proletariat, and particularly a part of the Bourgeois-ideologists, or middle-class thinkers, who have attained a theoretical knowledge of the whole historical movement.

The Proletariat is the only truly revolutionary Class amongst the present enemies of the Bourgeoisie. All the other classes of Society are being destroyed by the modern industrial system, the Proletariat is its peculiar product.

The small manufacturers, shopkeepers, proprietors, peasants, &c., all fight against the Bourgeoisie, in order to defend their position as small Capitalists. They are, therefore, not revolutionary, but conservative. They are even reactionary, for they attempt to turn backwards the chariot wheels of History. When these subordinate classes are revolutionary, they are so with reference to their necessary absorption into the Proletariat; they defend their future, not their present, interests—they leave their own Class point of view to take up that of the Proletariat.

The Mob—this product of the decomposition of the lowest substrata of the old Social system—is partly forced into the revolutionary Proletarian movement. The social position of this portion of the people makes it, however, in general a ready and venal tool for Reactionist intrigues.

The vital conditions of Society, as at present constituted, no longer exist for the Proletariat. Its very existence is a flagrant contradiction to those conditions. The Proletarian has no property; the relation in which he stands to his family has nothing in common with Middle-class family relationships; the modern system of industrial labour, the modern slavery of Labour under Capital, which obtains in England as in France, in America as in Germany, has robbed him of his National Character. Law, Morality, Religion, are for him so many Middle-class prejudices, under which so many Middle-class interests are concealed.

All the hitherto dominant Classes, have tried to preserve the position they had already attained, by imposing the conditions under which they possessed and increased their possessions, upon the rest of Society. But the Proletarians can gain possession of the Productive power of Society—of the instruments of Labour,—only by annihilating their own, hitherto acknowledged mode of appropriation. The Proletarians have nothing of their own to secure, their task is to destroy all previously existing private securities and possessions.

All the historical movements hitherto recorded were the movements of minorities, or movements in the interest of minorities. The Proletarian movement is the independent movement of the immense majority in favour of the immense majority. The Proletariat, the lowest stratum of existing society, cannot arouse, cannot rise without causing the complete disruption and dislocation of all the superincumbent classes.

Though the struggle of the Proletariat against the Bourgeoisie is not a National struggle in its Content—or Reality—it is so in its Form. The Proletarians of every country must settle accounts with the Bourgeoisie there.

While we have thus sketched the general aspect presented by the development of the Proletariat, we have followed the more or less concealed Civil War pervading existing Society, to the point where it must break forth in an open Revolution, and where the Proletarians arrive at the supremacy of their own class through the violent fall of the Bourgeoisie.

We have seen, that all previous forms of Society have rested upon the antagonism of oppressing and oppressed Classes. But in order to oppress a Class, the conditions under which it can continue at least its enslaved existence must be secured. The Serf in the Middle Ages, even within his serfdom, could better his condition and become a member of the Commune; the burghers could become a Middle-class under the yoke of feudal Monarchy. But the modern Proletarian, instead of improving his condition with the development of modern Industry, is daily sinking deeper and deeper even below the conditions of existence of his own Class. The Proletarian tends to become a pauper, and Pauperism is more rapidly developed than population and Wealth. From this it appears, that the Middle-class is incapable of remaining any longer the ruling Class of Society, and of compelling Society to adopt the conditions of Middle-class existence as its own vital conditions. This Class is incapable of governing, because it is incapable of ensuring the bare existence of its Slaves, even within the limits of their slavery, because it is obliged to keep them, instead of being kept by them. Society can no longer exist under this Class, that is, its existence is no longer compatible with that of Society.

The most indispensable condition for the existence and supremacy of the Bourgeoisie, is the accumulation of Wealth in the hands of private individuals, the formation and increase of Capital. The condition upon which Capital depends is the Wages-system, and this system again, is founded upon the Competition of the Proletarians with each other. But the progress of the modern industrial system, towards which the Bourgeoisie lend an unconscious and involuntary support, tends to supersede the isolated position of Proletarians by the revolutionary Union of their Class, and to replace Competition by Association. The progress of the modern industrial system, therefore, cuts away, from under the feet of the Middle-class, the very ground upon which they produce and appropriate to themselves the produce of Labour. Thus the Bourgeoisie produce before all the men who dig their very grave. Their destruction and the victory of the Proletarians are alike unavoidable.

Chapter 2: Proletarians and Communists

What relationship subsists between the Communists and the Proletarians?

The Communists form no separate party in opposition to the other existing working-class parties.

They have no interest different from that of the whole Proletariat.

They lay down no particular principles according to which they wish to direct and to shape the Proletarian movement.

The Communists are distinguishable among the various sections of the Proletarian party on two accounts—namely, that in the different *national* Proletarian struggles, the Communists understand, and direct attention to, the common interest of the collective Proletariat, an interest independent of all nationality; and that, throughout the various phases of development assumed by the struggle between the Bourgeoisie and the Proletariat, the Communists always represent the interest of the Whole Movement.

In a word, the Communists are the most advanced, the most progressive section, among the Proletarian parties of all countries; and this section has a theoretical advantage, compared with the bulk of the Proletariat—it has obtained an insight into the historical conditions, the march, and the general results of the Proletarian Movement.

The more immediate aim of the Communists is that of all other Proletarian sections. *The organisation of the Proletariat as* a class, *the destruction of Middle-class supremacy, and the conquest of political power by the Proletarians.*

The theoretical propositions of the Communists are not based upon Ideas, or Principles, discovered by this or that Universal Reformer.

Their propositions are merely general expressions for the actual conditions, causes, &c., of an existing battle between certain classes, the conditions of an historical Movement which is going on before our very eyes. The abolition of existing conditions of Property does not form a distinguishing characteristic of Communism.

All such conditions have been subject to a continual change, to the operation of many historical Movements.

The French Revolution, for example, destroyed the feudal conditions of property, and replaced them by Bourgeois ones.

It is not, therefore, the *abolition of property generally* which distinguishes Communism; it is the *abolition of Bourgeois property.* But Modern Middle-class private property is the last and most perfect expression for that mode of Production and Distribution which rests on the antagonism of classes, on the using up of the many by the few.

In this sense, indeed, the Communists might resume their whole Theory in that single expression—The *abolition of private property.*

It has been reproached to us, the Communists, that we wish to destroy the property which is the product of a man's own labour; self-acquired property, the basis of all personal freedom, activity, and independence.

Self-acquired property! Do you mean the property of the small shopkeeper, small tradesman, small peasant, which precedes the present system of Middle-class property? We do not need to abolish that, the progress of industrial development is daily destroying it.

Or do you mean modern Middle-class property?

Does labour under the Wages-system create property for the Wages-slave, for the Proletarian? No. It creates Capital, that is, a species of property which plunders Wages-labour, for Capital can only increase on condition of creating a new supply of Wages-labour, in order to use it up anew. Property, in its present form, rests upon the antagonism of Capital and Wages-labour. Let us look at both sides of this antithesis. To be a Capitalist means to occupy not only a personal, but a social position in the system of production.

Capital is a collective product, and can be used and set in motion only by the common activity of many, or, to speak exactly, only by the united exertions of all the members of society.

Capital is thus not an individual, it is a social power.

Therefore, when Capital is changed into property belonging in common to all the members of society, personal property is not thereby changed into social property. It was social property before. The social character only of property, in such a case, is changed. Property loses its class character.

Let us now turn to Wages-labour.

The minimum rate of wages is the average price of Proletarian labour. And what is the minimum rate of wages? It is that quantity of produce which is necessary to conserve the working capacities of the labourer. What the Wages-slave can gain by his activity is merely what is requisite for the bare reproduction of his existence. We by no means wish to abolish this personal appropriation of the products of labour, an appropriation leaving no net profit, no surplus, to be applied to command the labour of others. We only wish to change the miserably insufficient character of this appropriation, whereby the producer lives only to increase Capital; that is, whereby he is kept alive only so far as it may be [in] the interest of the ruling class.

In Middle-class society, actual living labour is nothing but a means of increasing accumulated labour. In Communistic society, accumulated labour is only a means of enlarging, increasing, and varifying the vital process of the producers.

In Middle-class society, the Past reigns over the Present. In Communistic society, the Present reigns over the Past. In Middle-class society, Capital is independent and personal, while the active individual is dependent and deprived of personality.

And the destruction of such a system is called by Middle-class advocates, the destruction of personality and freedom. They are so far right, that the question in hand is the destruction of Middle-class personality, independence, and freedom.

Within the present Middle-class conditions of production, freedom means free trade, freedom of buying and selling. But if trade, altogether, is to fall, so will free trade fall with the rest. The declamations about free trade, as all the remaining Bourgeois declamations upon the subject of freedom generally, have a meaning only when opposed to fettered trade, and to the enslaved tradesmen of the Middle Ages; they have no meaning whatever in reference to the Communistic destruction of profit-mongering, of the Middle-class conditions of production, and of the Middle-class itself.

You are horrified that we aim at the abolition of private property. But under your present system of society, private property has no existence for nine-tenths of its members; its existence is based upon the very fact that it exists not at all for nine-tenths of the population. You reproach us, then, that we aim at the abolition of a species of property which involves, as a necessary condition, the absence of all property for the immense majority of society. In a word, you reproach us that we aim at the destruction of *your* property. That is precisely what we aim at.

From the moment when Labour can no longer be changed into Capital,—into money, or rent,—into a social power capable of being *monopolised,* that is, from the moment when personal property can no longer constitute itself as Middle-class property, from that moment you declare that human personality is abolished.

You acknowledge, then, that for you personality generally means the personality of the Bourgeois, the Middle-class proprietor. It is precisely this kind of personality which is to be destroyed.

Communism deprives no one of the right of appropriating social products; it only takes away from him the power of appropriating the command over the labour of others.

It has been objected that activity will cease, and a universal laziness pervade society, were the abolition of private property once accomplished.

According to this view of the matter, Middle-class society ought, long since, to have been ruined through idleness; for under the present system, those who do work acquire no property, and those who acquire property do no work. This objection rests upon the tautological proposition, that there will be no Wages-labour whenever there is no Capital.

All the objections made to the Communistic mode of producing and distributing physical products, have also been directed against the production and distribution of intellectual products. As, in the opinion of the Bourgeois, the destruction of class property involves the cessation of appropriation, in like manner the cessation of class-civilisation, in his opinion, is identical with the cessation of civilisation generally.

The civilisation whose loss he deplores, is the system of civilising men into machines.

But do not dispute with us, while you measure the proposed abolition of Middle-class property, by your Middle-class ideas of freedom, civilisation, jurisprudence, and the like. Your ideas are the necessary consequences of the Middle-class conditions of property and production, as your jurisprudence is the Will of your class raised to the dignity of Law, a Will whose subject is given in the economical conditions of your class.

The selfish mode of viewing the question, whereby you confound your transitory conditions of production and property with the eternal laws of Reason and Nature, is common to all ruling classes. What you understand with regard to Antique and Feudal property, you cannot understand with regard to modern Middle-class property.—The destruction of domestic ties! Even the greatest Radicals are shocked at this scandalous intention of the Communists.

Upon what rests the present system, the Bourgeois system of family relationships? Upon Capital, upon private gains, on profit-mongering. In its most perfect form it exists only for the Bourgeoisie, and it finds a befitting compliment in the compulsory celibacy of the Proletarians, and in public prostitution.

The Bourgeois family system naturally disappears with the disappearance of its complement, and the destruction of both is involved in the destruction of Capital.

Do you reproach us that we intend abolishing the using up of children by their parents? We acknowledge this crime.

Or that we will abolish the most endearing relationships, by substituting a public and social system of education for the existing private one?

And is not your system of education also determined by society? By the social conditions, within the limits of which you educate? by the more or less direct influence of society, through the medium of your schools, and so forth? The Communists do not invent the influence of society upon education; they only seek to change its character, to rescue education from the influence of a ruling class.

Middle-class talk about domestic ties and education, about the endearing connection of parent and child, becomes more and more disgusting in proportion as the family ties of the Proletarians are torn asunder, and their children changed into machines, into articles of commerce, by the extension of the modern industrial system.

But you intend introducing a community of women, shrieks the whole Middle-class like a tragic chorus.

The Bourgeois looks upon his wife as a mere instrument of production; he is told that the instruments of production are to be used up in common, and thus he naturally supposes that women will share the common fate of other machines.

He does not even dream that it is intended, on the contrary, to abolish the position of woman as a mere instrument of production.

For the rest, nothing can be more ludicrous than the highly moral and religious horror entertained by the Bourgeoisie towards the pretended official community of women among the Communists. We do not require to introduce community of women, it has always existed.

Your Middle-class gentry are not satisfied with having the wives and daughters of their Wages-slaves at their disposal—not to mention the innumerable public prostitutes—but they take a particular pleasure in seducing each other's wives.

Middle-class marriage is in reality a community of wives. At the most, then, we could only be reproached for wishing to substitute an open, above-board community of women, for the present mean, hypocritical, sneaking kind of community. But it is evident enough that with the disappearance of the present conditions of production, the community of women occasioned by them—namely, official and non-official prostitution—will also disappear.

The Communists are further reproached with desiring to destroy patriotism, the feeling of Nationality.

The Proletarian has no Fatherland. You cannot deprive him of that which he has not got. When the Proletariat obtains political supremacy, becomes the National Class, and constitutes it-self as the Nation—it will, indeed, be national, though not in the middle-class sense of the word.

The National divisions and antagonisms presented by the European Nations, already tend towards obliteration through the development of the Bourgeoisie, through the influence of free trade, a worldwide market, the uniformity of the modern modes of Production and the conditions of modern life arising out of the present industrial system.

The supremacy of the Proletariat will hasten this obliteration of national peculiarities, for the united action of—at least—all civilized countries is one of the first conditions of Proletarian emancipation.

In proportion to the cessation of the using up of one individ-ual by another, will be the cessation of the using up of one nation by another. The hostile attitude assumed by nations towards each other, will cease with the antagonisms of the classes into which each nation is divided.

The accusations against communism, which have been made from the Theological, Philosophical, and Ideological, points of view, deserve no further notice.

Does it require any great degree of intellect to perceive that changes occur in our ideas, conceptions, and opinions, in a word, that the *consciousness* of man alters with every change in the conditions of his physical existence, in his social relations and position?

Does not the history of Ideas show, that intellectual produc-tion has always changed with the changes in material produc-tion? The ruling ideas of any age have always been the ideas of the then ruling class.

You talk of ideas which have revolutionised society; but you merely express the fact, that within the old form of society, the elements of a new one were being formed, and that the dissolu-tion of the old ideas was keeping pace with the dissolution of the old conditions of social life.

When the antique world was in its last agony, Christianity triumphed over the antique religion. When the dogmas of Chris-tianity were superseded by the enlightenment of the eighteenth century, feudal society was concentrating its last efforts against the then revolutionary Bourgeoisie. The ideas of religious liberty and freedom of thought were the expressions of unlimited competition in the affairs and free trade in the sphere of intellect and religion.

But you say, theological, moral, philosophical, political and legal ideas, are subject to be modified by the progress of historical development. Religion, ethics, philosophy, politics, and jurisprudence are, however, of all times. And we find, besides certain eternal ideas, for example, Freedom, Justice, and the like—which are common to all the various social phases and states. But communism destroys these eternal truths; it pretends to abolish religion and Ethics, instead of merely giving them a new form; Communism, therefore, contradicts all preceding modes of historical development.

To what does this accusation amount? The history of all preceding states of society is simply the history of class antagonisms, which were fought under different conditions, and assumed different forms during the different historical epochs.

Whatever form these antagonisms may have assumed, the using up of one part of society by another part, is a fact, common to the whole past. No wonder then, that the social consciousness of past ages should have a common ground, in spite of the multiplicity and diversity of social arrangements: that it should move in certain common forms of thinking, which will completely disappear with the disappearance of class antagonism.

The communistic revolution is the most thorough-going rupture, with the traditionary conditions of property, no wonder then, that its progress will involve the completest rupture with traditionary ideas.

But we must have done with the middle-class accusations against communism.

We have seen that the first step in the proletarian revolution, will be the conquest of Democracy, the *elevation of the Proletariat to the state of the ruling class.*

The Proletarians will use their political supremacy in order to deprive the middle-class of the command of capital; to centralise all the instruments of production in the hands of the State, that is, in those of the whole proletariat organized as the ruling class, and to increase the mass of productive power with the utmost possible rapidity.

It is a matter of course that this can be done, at first, only by despotic interference with the rights of property, and middle-class conditions of production. By regulations, in fact, which—economically considered—appear insufficient and untenable; which, therefore, in the course of the revolution, necessitate ulterior and more radical measures, and are unavoidable as a means towards a thorough change in the modes of production.

These regulations will, of course, be different in different countries. But for the most advanced countries, the following will be pretty generally applicable:

1. The national appropriation of the land, and the application of rent to the public revenue.
2. A heavy progressive tax.
3. Abolition of the right of inheritance.
4. Confiscation of the property of all emigrants and rebels.
5. Centralization of credit in the hands of the State, by means of a national bank, with an exclusive monopoly and a state-capital.
6. Centralization of all the means of communication in the hands of the state.
7. Increase of the national manufactories; of the instruments of production; the cultivation of waste lands and the improvement of the land generally according to a common plan.
8. Labour made compulsory for all; and the organization of industrial armies, especially for agriculture.
9. The union of manufacturing and agricultural industry; with a view of gradually abolishing the antagonism between town and country.
10. The public and gratuitous education of all children; the abolition of the present system of factory labour for children; the conjunction of education and material production with other regulations of a similar nature.

When Class distinctions will have finally disappeared, and production will have been concentrated in the hands of this

Association which comprises the whole nation, the public power will lose its political character. Political power in the exact sense of the word, being the organised power of one class, which enables it to oppress another. When the proletariat has been forced to unite as a class during its struggle with the Bourgeoisie, when it has become the ruling class by a revolution, and as such has destroyed, by force, the old conditions of production, it destroys, necessarily, with these conditions of production, the conditions of existence of all class antagonism, of classes generally, and thus it destroys, also, its own supremacy as a class. The old Bourgeois Society, with its classes, and class antagonisms, will be replaced by an association, wherein the *free development of* each is *the condition of the free development of* all.

Chapter 3: Socialist and Communist Literature

I. Reactionary Socialism

a. Feudal Socialism

The historical position of the French and English Aristocracy devolved upon them, at a certain period, the task of writing pamphlets against the social system of the modern Bourgeoisie. These Aristocracies were again beaten by a set of detestable parvenus and nobodies in the July days of 1830, and in the English Reform Bill movement. There could be no longer any question about a serious political struggle. There remained only the possibility of conducting a literary combat. But even in the territory of Literature, the old modes of speech, current during the Restoration, had become impossible.

In order to exite sympathy, the Aristocracy had to assume the semblance of disinterestedness, and to draw up their accusation of the Bourgeoisie, apparently as advocates for the used-up Proletarians. The Aristocracy thus revenged themselves on their new masters—by lampoons and fearful prophecies of coming woe.

In this way feudal socialism arose—half lamentation, half libel, half echo of the Past, half prophecy of a threatening Future—sometimes striking the very heart of the Bourgeoisie by its sarcastic, bitter judgments, but always accompanied by a certain tinge of the ludicrous, from its complete inability to comprehend the march of modern history.

The Feudal Socialists waved the Proletarian alms-bag aloft, to assemble the people around them. But as often as the people came, they perceived upon the hind parts of these worthies, the old feudal arms and quarterings, and abandoned them with noisy and irreverent hilarity. A part of the French Legitimists and the party of Young England played this farce.

When the Feudalists show that their mode of exploitation (*using up* one *class by another*) was different from the Bourgeois mode, they forget that their mode was practicable only under circumstances and conditions which have passed away—never to return. When they show that the modern Proletariat never existed under their supremacy, they simply forget that the modern Bourgeoisie is the necessary offspring of their own social order.

For the rest, they so little conceal the reactionary nature of their criticism, that their chief reproach against the Bourgeois-regime is that of having created a class which is destined to annihilate the old social forms and arrangements altogether.

It is not so much that the Bourgeoisie [has] created a Proletariat, but that this Proletariat is revolutionary.

Hence, in their political practice, they take part in all reactionary measures against the working classes; and in ordinary life, despite their grandiloquent phrases, they condescend to gather the golden apples, and to give up chivalry, true love, and honour for the traffic in wool, butcher's meat, and corn.

As the parson has always gone hand-in-hand with the landlord, so has Priestly Socialism with Feudal Socialism.

Nothing is easier than to give Christian ascetism a tinge of Socialism. Has not Christianity itself vociferated against private property, marriage, and the powers that be? Have not charity, and mendicity, celibacy and mortification of the flesh, monastic life, and the supremacy of the Church been held up in the place of these things? Sacred Socialism is merely the holy water, with which the priest besprinkles the impotent wrath of the Aristocracy.

b. Shopocrat-Socialism[3]

The Feudal Aristocracy are not the only class who are, or will be, destroyed by the Bourgeoisie. Not the only class, the conditions of whose existence become exhausted and disappear, under the modern middle-class system. The mediaeval burgesses and yeoman were the precursors of the modern middle-class. In countries possessing a small degree of industrial and commercial development, this intermediate class still vegetates side by side with the nourishing Bourgeoisie.

In countries where modern civilization has been developed, a new intermediate class has been formed; floating as it were, between the Bourgeoisie and the Proletariat; and always renewing itself as a component part of Bourgeois society. Yet, the persons belonging to this class are constantly forced by competition downwards into the Proletariat, and the development of the modern industrial system will bring about the time when this small capitalist class will entirely disappear, and be replaced by managers and stewards, in commerce, manufactures, and agriculture.

In countries like France, where far more than one half of the population are small freeholders, it was natural, that writers who took part with the Proletariat against the Bourgeoisie, should measure the Bourgeois-regime by the small-capitalist standard; and should envisage the Proletarian question from the small-capitalist point of view. In this way arose the system of Shopocrat Socialism. Sismondi is the head of this school, in England as well as in France.

This school of socialism has dissected with great acuteness the modern system of production, and exposed the fallacies contained therein. It unveiled the hypocritical evasions of the political economists. It irrefutably demonstrated the destructive effects of machinery, and the division of labour; the concentration of capital and land in a few hands; over production; commercial crisis; the necessary destruction of the small capitalist; the misery of the Proletariat; anarchy in production, and scandalous inequality in the distribution of wealth; the destructive industrial wars of one nation with another; and the disappearance of old manners and customs, of patriarchal family arrangements, and of old nationalities.

But in its practical application, this Shopocrat, or Small-Capitalist Socialism, wish either to re-establish the old modes of production and traffic, and with these, the old conditions of property, and old society altogether—or forcibly to confine the modern means of production and traffic within the limits of these antique conditions of property, which were actually destroyed, necessarily so, by these very means. In both cases, Shopocrat Socialism is, at the same time reactionary and Utopian.

Corporations and guilds in manufactures, patriarchal idyllic arrangements in agriculture, are its beau ideal. This kind of Socialism has run to seed, and exhausted itself in silly lamentations over the past.

c. German (or "True") Socialism[4]

The Socialist and Communist literature of France originated under the Bourgeois-regime, and was the literary expression of the struggle against middle-class supremacy. It was introduced into Germany at a time when the Bourgeoisie there had began their battle against Feudal despotism.

German Philosophers—half-philosophers, and would-be literati—eagerly seized on this literature, and forgot that with the immigration of these French writings into Germany, the advanced state of French society, and of French class-struggles, had not, as a matter of course, immigrated along with them. This French literature, when brought into contact with the German phasis of social development, lost all its immediate practical significance, and assumed a purely literary aspect. It could appear in no other way than as an idle speculation upon the best possible state of society, upon the realization of the true nature of man. In a similar manner, the German philosophers of the eighteenth century, considered the demands of the first French Revolution as the demands of "Practical Reason" in its general sense, and the will of the revolutionary French bourgeoisie, was for them the law of the pure will, of volition as it ought to be; the law of man's inward nature.

The all-engrossing problem for the German literati was to bring the new French ideas into accordance with their old philosophic conscience; or rather, to appropriate the French ideas without leaving the philosophic point of view.

This appropriation took place in the same way as one masters a foreign language; namely, by translation.

It is known how the Monks of the middle-ages treated the manuscripts of the Greek and Roman classics. They wrote silly Catholic legends over the original text. The German literati did the very reverse, with respect to the profane French literature. They wrote their philosophical nonsense behind the French original. For example, behind the French critique of the modern money-system, they wrote "Estrangement of Human Nature"; behind the French critique of the bourgeois-regime, they wrote, "Destruction of the Supremacy of the Absolute," and so forth.

They baptized this interpolation of their philosophic modes of speech, with the French ideas by various names; "Philosophy in Action," True Socialism," The German Philosophy of Socialism," "Philosophical Foundation of Socialism," and the like.

The socialist and communist literature of France was completely emasculated. And when it had ceased, in German hands, to express the struggle of one class against another, the Germans imagined they had overcome French one-sidedness. They imagined they represented, not true interests and wants, but the interests and wants of abstract truth; not the proletarian interest, but the interest of human nature, as man as belonging to no class, a native of no merely terrestial countries—of man, belonging of the misty, remote region of philosophical imagination.

This German socialism, which composed its clumsy school themes with such exemplary solemnity, and then cried them along the street, gradually lost its pedantic and primitive innocence.

The battle of the German, particularly of the Prussian bourgeoisie, against feudalism and absolute monarchy, in a word, the liberal movement, became more serious.

True socialism had now the desired opportunity of placing socialist demands in opposition to the actual political movement; of hurling the traditionary second-hand Anathemas against liberalism, constitutional governments, bourgeois competition and free trade, bourgeois freedom of the press, bourgeois juries, bourgeois freedom and equality; the opportunity of preaching to the masses that they had nothing to gain and every thing to lose by this middle-class movement. German socialism forgot, very opportunely, that the French polemics, whose unmeaning echo it was—presupposed the modern middle-class system of society, with the corresponding physical conditions of social existence, and a suitable political constitution presupposed, in fact, the very things which had no existence in Germany, and which were the very things to be obtained by the middle-class movement.

German socialism was used by the German despots and their followers, priests, schoolmasters, bureaucrats, and bullfrog country squires—as a scarecrow to frighten the revolutionary middle-class.

It was the agreeable finish to the grapeshot, and cat o' nine tails, with which these Governments replied to the first proletarian insurrections of Germany.

While "true socialism" was thus employed in assisting the Governments against the German bourgeoisie, it also directly represented a reactionary interest, that of the German small capitalists and shopocracy. In Germany the real social foundation of the existing state of things, was this class, remaining since the 16th century, and always renewing itself under slightly different forms.

Its preservation was the preservation of the existing order of things in Germany. The industrial and political supremacy of the bourgeoisie involved the annihilation of this intermediate class; on the one hand, by the centralisation of capital; on the other, by the creation of a revolutionary proletariat. German, or "true" socialism, appeared to this shopocracy as a means of killing two birds with one stone. It spread like an epidemic.

The robe of speculative cobwebs, adorned with rhetorical flourishes and sickly sentimentalism—in which the German socialists wrapped the dry bones of their eternal, absolute truths, increased the demand for their commodity among this public.

And the German socialists were not wanting in due appreciation of their mission, to be the grandiloquent representatives of the German shopocrats.

They proclaimed the German nation to be the archetypal nation; the German cockneys, to be archetypal men. They gave every piece of cockney rascality a hidden socialist sense, whereby it *was* interpreted to mean the reverse of rascality. They reached the limits of their system, when they directly opposed the destructive tendency of communism, and proclaimed their own sublime indifference towards all class-antagonism. With very few exceptions, all the so-called socialist and communist publications which circulate in Germany emanate from this school, and are enervating filthy trash.

II. Conservative (or Bourgeois) Socialism

A part of the Bourgeoisie desires to alleviate social dissonances, with a view of securing the existence of middle-class society.

To this section belong economists, philanthropists, humanitarians, improvers of the condition of the working classes, patrons of charitable institutions, cruelty-to-animals-bill supporters, temperance advocates, in a word, hole and corner reformers of the most varied and piebald aspect. This middle-class Socialism has even been developed into complete systems.

As an example, we may cite Proudhon's Philosophy of Poverty.

The socialist bourgeois wish to have the vital conditions of modern society without the accompanying struggles and dangers. They desire the existing order of things, minus the revolutionary and destructive element contained therein. They wish to have a bourgeoisie without a proletariat. The bourgeoisie, of course, consider the world wherein they reign, to be the best possible world. Bourgeois socialism develops this comfortable hypothesis into a complete system. When these socialists urge the proletariat to realise their system, to march towards the New Jerusalem, they ask in reality, that the proletariat should remain within the limits of existing society, and yet lay aside all bitter and unfavourable opinions concerning it.

A second, less systematic, and more practical school of middle-class socialists, try to hinder all revolutionary movements among the producers, by teaching them that their condition cannot be improved by this or that political change—but only by a change in the material conditions of life, in the economical arrangements of society. Yet, by a change in the modern life-conditions, these socialists do not mean the abolition of the middle-class modes of production and distribution, attainable only in a revolutionary manner, they mean administrative reforms, to be made within the limits of the old system, which, therefore, will leave the relation of capital and wages-labour untouched—and, at most, will merely simplify the details and diminish the cost of bourgeois government.

This kind of socialism finds its most fitting expression in empty rhetorical flourishes.

Free Trade! for the benefit of the working classes. A tariff! for the benefit of the working classes.

Isolated imprisonment and the silent system! for the benefit of the working classes.

This last phrase is the only sincere and earnest one, among the whole stock in trade of the middle-class socialists. Their socialism consists in affirming, that the bourgeois is a bourgeois . . . for the benefit of the working classes!

III. Critical Utopian Socialism and Communism

We do not speak here of the literature, which, in all the great revolutions of modern times, has expressed the demands of the proletariat: as leveller pamphleteers, the writings of Babeuf and others.[5]

The first attempts of the proletariat towards directly forwarding its own class-interest, made during the general movement which overthrew feudal society, necessarily failed—by reason of the crude, undeveloped form of the proletariat itself; as well as by the want of those material conditions for its emancipation, which are but the product of the bourgeois-epoch. The revolutionary literature, which accompanied this first movement of the proletariat, had necessarily a reactionary content. It taught a universal asceticism and a rude sort of equality.

The Socialist and communist systems, properly so called, the systems of St. Simon, Owen, Fourier and others, originated in the early period of the struggle between the proletariat and the bourgeoisie, which we described in chap. 1.

The inventors of these systems perceived the fact of class-antagonism, and the activity of the dissolvent elements within the prevailing social system. But they did not see any spontaneous historical action, any characteristic political movement, on the part of the proletariat.

And because the development of class-antagonism keeps pace with the development of the industrial system, they could not find the material conditions for the emancipation of the proletariat; they were obliged to seek for a social science, for social laws, in order to create those conditions.

Their personal inventive activity took the place of social activity, imaginary conditions of proletarian emancipation were substituted for the historical ones, and a subjective, fantastic organisation of society, for the gradual and progressive organisation of the proletariat as a class. The approaching phasis of universal history resolved itself, for them, into the propagandism and practical realisation of their peculiar social plans.

They had, indeed, the consciousness of advocating the interest of the producers as the most suffering class of society. The proletariat existed for them, only under this point of view of the most oppressed class.

The undeveloped state of the class-struggle, and their own social position, induced these socialists to believe they were removed far above class-antagonism. They desired to improve the position of all the members of society, even of the most favoured. Hence, their continual appeals to the whole of society, even to the dominant class. You have only to understand their system, in order to see it is the best possible plan for the best possible state of society.

Hence too, they reject all political, and particularly all revolutionary action, they desire to attain their object in a peaceful manner, and try to prepare the way for the new social gospel, by the force of example, by small, isolated experiments, which, of course, cannot but turn out signal *failures.*

This fantastic representation of future society expressed the feeling of a time when the proletariat was quite undeveloped, and had quite an imaginary conception of its own position—it was the expression of an instinctive want for a universal social revolution.

There are, however, critical elements contained in all these socialist and communist writings. They attack the foundation of existing society. Hence they contain a treasure of materials for the enlightenment of the Producers. Their positive propositions regarding a future state of society; e.g. abolition of the antagonism of town and country, of family institutions, of individual accumulation, of wages-labour, the proclamation of social harmony, the change of political power into a mere superintendence of production—all these propositions expressed the abolition of class-antagonism, when this last was only commencing its evolution; and, therefore, they have, with these authors a purely Utopian sense.

The importance of critical-Utopian Socialism and Communism, stands in an inverted proportion to the progress of the historical movement. In proportion as the class-battle is evolved and assumes a definite form, so does this imaginary elevation over it, this fantastic resistance to it, lose all practical worth, all theoretical justification. Hence, it happens, that although the originators of these systems were revolutionary in various respects, yet their followers have invariably formed reactionary sects. They hold fast by their master's old dogmas and doctrines, in opposition to the progressive historical evolution of the Proletariat. They seek, therefore, logically enough, to deaden class opposition, to mediate between the extremes. They still dream of the experimental realization of their social Utopias through isolated efforts—the founding of a few phalanteres, of a few home colonies, of a small Icaria,—a duodecimo edition of the New Jerusalem; and they appeal to the philanthropy of Bourgeois hearts and purses for the building expenses of these air-castles and chimeras. They gradually fall back into the category of the above mentioned reactionary or conservative Socialists, and distinguish themselves from these only by their more systematic pedantry, by their fanatical faith in the miraculous powers of their Social panacea.

Hence, they violently oppose all political movements in the Proletariat, which indeed, can only be occasioned by a blind and wilful disbelief in the new Gospel. In France, the Fourierists oppose the Reformists; in England, the Owenites react against the Chartists.[6]

The Communists invariably support every revolutionary movement against the existing order of things, social and political.

But in all these movements, they endeavour to point out the property question, whatever degree of development, in every particular case, it may have obtained—as the leading question. The Communists labour for the union and association of the revolutionary parties of all countries. The Communists disdain to conceal their opinions and ends. They openly declare, that these ends can be attained only by the overthrow of all hitherto existing social arrangements. Let the ruling classes tremble at a Communist Revolution. The Proletarians have nothing to lose in it save their chains. They will gain a World. Let the Proletarians of all countries unite!

Notes

1. The following sentence from the *Manifesto* were omitted in Macfarlane's translation: "To this end, Communists of various nationalities have assembled in London and sketched the following manifesto, to be published in the English, French, German, Italian, Flemish and Danish languages." (Samuel Moore translation 1888)

2. The chapter heading "Bourgeois and Proletarians" is omitted, as is a sentence at the beginning of the first paragraph: "The history of all hitherto existing society is the history of class struggles." (Moore translation)

3. Macfarlane footnote: "The term in the original is *Kleinburger,* meaning smail burghers, or citizens. A class, comprising small capitalists generally, whether small farmers, small manufacturers, or retail shopkeepers. As these last form the predominant element of this class in England. I have chosen the term *Shopocrat* to express the German term."

4. Macfarlane footnote: "It was the set of writers characterized in the following chapter, who themselves called their theory "TRUE SOCIALISM"; if, therefore, after perusing this chapter, the reader should not agree with them as to the name, this is no fault of the authors of the Manifesto."

5. Marx and Engels's original refers to "Babeuf and others" but makes no reference to the English Levellers.

6. Macfarlane footnote: "It is not to be forgotten that these lines were written before the revolution of February, and that the examples have, accordingly, reference to the state of parties of that time."

In the German original there is a final section heading here ("POSI-TION OF THE COMMUNISTS TO THE VARIOUS EXISTING OPPOSITION PARTIES") which is followed by:

The Communists fight for the attainment of the immediate aims, for the enforcement of the momentary interests of the working class; but in the movement of the present, they also represent and take care of the future of that movement. In France, the Communists ally with the Social Democrats against the conservative and radical bourgeoisie, reserving, however, the right to take up a critical position in regard to phases and illusions traditionally handed down from the Great Revolution.

In Switzerland, they support the Radicals, without losing sight of the fact that this party consists of antagonistic elements, partly of Democratic Socialists, in the French sense, partly of radical bourgeois.

In Poland, they support the party that insists on an agrarian revolution as the prime condition for national emancipation, that party which fomented the insurrection of Krakow in 1846.

In Germany, they fight with the bourgeoisie whenever it acts in a revolutionary way, against the absolute monarchy, the feudal squirearchy, and the petty-bourgeoisie.

But they never cease, for a single instant, to instill into the working class the clearest possible recognition of the hostile antagonism between bourgeoisie and proletariat, in order that the German workers may straightway use, as so many weapons against the bourgeoisie, the social and political conditions that the bourgeoisie must necessarily introduce along with its supremacy, and in order that, after the fall of the reactionary classes in Germany, the fight against the bourgeoisie itself may immediately begin.

The Communists turn their attention chiefly to Germany, because that country is on the eve of a bourgeois revolution that is bound to be carried out under more advanced conditions of European civilization and with a much more developed proletariat than that of England was in the seventeenth, and France in the eighteenth century, and because the bourgeois revolution in Germany will be but the prelude to an immediately following proletarian revolution. [Moore Translation]

Index

About the Author

David Black is a freelance author and journalist who writes about history, politics, culture, and philosophy. His previous book, *Acid: A New Secret History of LSD*, was published in 2002. He lives in London.